Successful Job Search and Interview Preparation

2-in-1 Book

Learn The Secrets of Job Hunting, Ace that Interview and Get Your Dream Job, Even if You've Been Searching for a Long Time With no Luck

Successful Job Search

Feel Like a Lost Fish in The Middle of the Immense "Job Hunting" Ocean? Discover The Best Tools and Proven Techniques to Land Your Dream Job in Today's Competitive Market

Table of Contents

INTRODUCTION 7

Chapter 1 - The Hunt Begins 10

   Seven Simple Ways to Find the Job You Love. 11

   Using the Internet to Find Your Dream Job 15

   How to Find Jobs that Aren't Advertised. 17

Chapter 2—A Resume to Beat Them All 20

   Creating a Killer Resume. 20

   How to Tailor Your Resume to a Specific Job. 24

   How to Write Great Cover Letters. 26

Chapter 3 - Get Ahead with an Online Portfolio 32

   The Lowdown on Creating an Irresistible LinkedIn Profile. 36

   How a Blog Can Boost Your Career. 40

   Six Fabulous Tools to Help You Put Together Your Online Portfolio. 41

Chapter 5—Shameless Self-Promotion 54

Chapter 6—Breaking Barriers 64

Chapter 7—Job Interview Secrets 75

Chapter 8—Make It Happen 85

Conclusion 92

INTRODUCTION

Finding the job that is right for you can be a difficult, complicated, and sometimes stressful process. Whether you are looking for your first job, a better job, or a career change job, you'll need to develop a plan on how to do so and then you'll need to find out the best ways to get that job you're looking for. Many people have job or career aspirations, but they get stuck at where they're at because they don't have a clue on how to get that job or career.

In this book, I'm going to provide you with the tools and tips you'll need to get the job you want. I'll tell you how you can find those jobs, whether they are advertised or not. I will also tell you how to position yourself above other candidates who are applying for the same job.

My name is David Allen. I am a how-to-get-a-job expert. I've had years of experience as a human resource director for multiple companies in different industries. I have also worked as a recruiter, recruiting people to fill various corporate job openings. And, finally, I have worked as a job consultant, helping people find their optimum jobs. Over the years, I have accumulated a lot of knowledge regarding the best way for people to get the jobs in which they're interested. In my experiences, I've found that many people do not know how to go about getting their dream job and, as a result, they never knew that an opening for that job existed, or they didn't know how to place themselves in a position to get the job they would have loved to have had. People I have worked with in my human resources, recruiting and counseling positions have often encouraged me to write a book and share my vast knowledge and years of experience with others who could benefit from it. With that in mind, I've written this book.

If you'll just take the time to read this book, and if you'll use the tips and suggestions which apply to your particular situation, you'll have a great chance to get the job you want. Through the years, I have helped people get jobs or careers they never thought they'd have a chance to get. Depending on the career you are interested in and the level you are at with your own job experiences, each career or job requires a different approach. There is not one single way to find the job you want. Cookie-cutter approaches and job-hunting templates don't work, as each industry, each job, each employer is different. That's why I intend to give you a number of ways to find and get the dream job you are looking for. After reading this book, you will also find that you'll be more efficient in your job search. You'll learn where to look for jobs, how to look for jobs, and then to go after the jobs you're interested in. Not only will this information save you time, it will also give you a better chance to secure the job in which you're interested and place you above the clutter of applicants for the same position.

As a career counselor, I have been able to help many people find jobs or careers that suit them. Whether they were looking to make more money, utilize their talents, or find a work environment or career that better suited them, I've been able to point them in the right direction and counsel them on how they might go about achieving success as they search for the job or career of their choice. I've received thanks from people who maintain that the help I provided was life-altering. I am hoping that I can do the same with you and, maybe one day, I will receive a testimonial from you telling me that you are forever grateful on how the tips in this book placed you on the right career path.

If you'll read this short book and if you'll implement the tips and techniques which apply to you, I can assure you that you'll have a chance to be your best self in finding the job you want. In my younger days, an old coffee buddy of mine and I would often talk about the dream jobs we wanted to have one day. Early on in our discussions, we determined something that still applies today: You will never be able to get that dream job if you don't apply for it. So, the moral of the story with job hunting is simple: You are very unlikely to get a job that you don't pursue. As an aside to that, how you pursue that job may well determine whether you get the job or not. If you read this book and follow the tips which are appropriate for you, you'll have the best chance of getting that job. No, I can't guarantee that you'll get any job you apply for, but I'll guarantee that you will have your best chance in getting that job.

I have a friend of mine who has written many self-help books and he is considered an expert in that field. He tells me that there are two kinds of people that will read self-help books such as this one. There are those that will read the books and place the tips and techniques on a backburner, often never getting back to them. Then there are those who read the books and implement immediately the tips and techniques they derive from the book. I'm sure you can guess which of the two types of readers are more successful. Hopefully, you'll find yourself in the group that implements the knowledge you gain immediately. This will give you the best chance of succeeding in your efforts to secure a new job.

The tips and techniques I'm providing in this book can provide incredible results, if you take the time and make the effort to implement them. Every chapter in this book is full of information on how you can go about getting the job you want. Let's get after it…together we can make it happen.

Chapter 1 - The Hunt Begins

Where do I start, you ask. Looking for a job can seem overwhelming, especially at the beginning of your search. This is why it will be important for you to develop a plan before you begin to apply for specific jobs or at specific companies. Here are some steps you can follow in preparing to find the job you really want.

Decide What You Want. There are tons of job openings out there for prospective employees to choose from. Before you place yourself into all this clutter, you should first ask yourself some questions that will help you define and refine the jobs you want to look for. What kind of job to you want to look for? (A marketing job, a sales job, a customer service job, etc.) Chances are that you'll already have a good idea as to what kind of job you are looking for. If not, I suggest that you get on some of the online job sites such as LinkedIn, Indeed, or Glassdoor, and browse the different categories to determine which type of jobs might appeal to you.

Also, you should determine what type of company you would like to work for. A large company, a small company, a medium-sized company or maybe it doesn't matter to you. Are you concerned with having a good working environment. If so, do any companies you're interested in have solid reputations for the working environment they provide? Have you had any previous experience which might be helpful to you in securing a job in any certain industry or company. As an example, the son of a friend of mine worked as a public relations person for a franchised restaurant chain. This was his first job out of college. He loved the restaurant industry, but he wanted to move from a public relations job to a marketing job. As a result, he decided to target restaurant chains (small and large) and franchised businesses (not just restaurants, but other franchised operations). This young man knew that his experience in restaurants and his experience with a franchised company could separate him from other applicants who did not have the same experience. So, in looking for a new job, it will be helpful to determine what previous experience you've had that might help you rise above other people who are applying for the same jobs.

Once you have determined the types of jobs you want and the types of companies you would like to work for, you'll want to develop a resume. In the next chapter of this book, I will outline specifically how you can develop a "killer" resume, however, before we do that, I'd like to give you some quick ideas on how you'll be using that resume.

Seven Simple Ways to Find the Job You Love.

1) **Social networks.** If you already have a presence on social media platforms such as Facebook, Twitter, and LinkedIn, those platforms can provide an excellent means for you to get the word out that you are looking for a job. The exception to that, of course, is if you already have a job and you want to keep it quiet that you are looking for another job. In that case, you won't want to use social networks to inform people that you are looking for a job. But if you are currently not employed or if you have a job and your current employer knows you are looking for another job, then social networks will provide a great way for you to get the word out. My thought on looking for jobs is that the person looking for the job should "Tell the World". I advise people to let as many people as possible know that you are looking for a job, as you never know who will be able to help you with that.

If you don't already have a Facebook or Twitter presence, then I doubt that establishing a presence on those platforms is going to help you with this job search. On the other hand, I strongly recommend that you establish a LinkedIn presence even if you don't have one now, as this could produce immediate results, possibly or probably from someone you don't even know now.

2) **Target companies directly.** Are there any companies in particular that you would really like to work for? Any companies that you think would be a great fit for you? If so, I suggest that you target those companies directly. You can do this in a number of different ways. The best way is probably to get on the company's web site. Many companies who have a web site, especially the larger companies, will feature job opportunities on their site. Often these job opportunities are posted on a page which you can access on a tab that is often labeled jobs or job opportunities, careers or career opportunities, or employment. These pages will allow you to determine if there are any current openings and what those openings are. If there are no openings in the field you're looking for and if you are really interested, I'd advise you not to get discouraged. Just because there are no openings today doesn't mean that there won't be an opening soon. If you really like the idea of working for this company, you might still send them a cover letter and resume, detailing specifically why you want to work for that company or why you think you would be a good fit. In these instances, I suggest that you specifically get the name of the person who would be responsible for hiring. For example, if you are interested in a marketing position, you should call the company and get the name, the proper title, and the correct spelling of the person who is in charge of the company's marketing department. Yes, you could do this in an email, but emails are very easy to delete and forget, so I would recommend that you use an old-fashioned letter sent through the US Post Office. Obviously, you won't want to do this for every company you apply to, however I encourage you to send to any specific companies in which you have interest and, if they don't have any current openings, ask them to keep on file for future reference whenever they have openings. I also found that something that is written or printed on paper is much more difficult to discard than an email which can be deleted with the simple click of a button.

And one other thing with these targeted letters and resumes. Unless their web site directs you otherwise, I would suggest that you send the letters to the person who will actually be in charge of the hiring. i.e.— For a marketing job, your letter would be better directed at the Vice President or Director of Marketing than it would be to the Human Resources Director. (Also, please note that there would be no harm in sending letters to both.)

3) **Use your school as a resource.** If you have any kind of post high school degree, whether it is a college degree, a technical or community college degree, a vocational or trade degree, you should know that those schools are very likely to have departments which can assist alumni in getting jobs. As most educational institutions like to frame their reputations on the jobs that their graduates get, they can be very helpful in referring alumni to job openings. By the same token, employers often use these school career centers to post job openings. A friend of mine who owns a small business has repeatedly hired employees from a nearby vocational school, as he knows that these employees are well-trained and also because he doesn't have to pay to advertise the job openings. And he also likes the fact that he will not be flooded with applications from people who have not had the proper training or who haven't refined their job search. For years, I have hired summer interns by contacting the nearby college and I have always been impressed with the selection of candidates they provide me with. So, whether you are looking for you first job after graduating from one of these post high school institutions or whether you have already had other jobs since your graduation, you should certainly consider them as a possible resource in finding your next job.

4) **Job fairs/career fairs.** Many colleges and universities, many communities and towns have job fairs in which employers have booths in which you can talk with representatives regarding job openings and opportunities. As someone who is looking for a job, these job fairs offer you the opportunity to meet with multiple employers, almost all of whom are hiring, and to find out what opportunities they might have available. They should be able to tell you what jobs there are specifically available and they will also be able to tell you how you might go about applying for a job there. If you are going to attend only of these job fairs, I suggest that you bring a supply of resumes that you can leave with any employers who you have interest in.

5) Get the word out…to everyone. This goes back to my "Tell the World" approach. If you're looking for a new job, I think it's important for you to tell as many people as possible about your interest in finding a new job. Again, you can never be sure who you might get an important referral from or an important parcel of information that will be helpful to you in getting the job you want. I know a woman who got important information about a job opening from the barista at her coffee shop. I know a man who got his foot in the door for his dream job by mentioning the fact that he wanted to get into a particular company at a birthday party for his niece. One of the in-laws there was a golfing buddy of one of the higher-ups in the company and, through this connection, the man who was looking for a job got an interview that he never would have been able to secure otherwise. Book clubs, parties, happy hours, volunteer activities—these all offer chances for you to spread the news that you are looking for a job.

Again, it should be pointed out that if you have a current job, you will probably have to be somewhat discreet in spreading the word that you are looking for another job, as you may not want that information to impact your current work situation.

6) Professional organizations, associations. You should also know that professional organizations or associations can be excellent sources for job openings in your particular field. Regardless of what profession or field you are in, there is probably an organization for the members of that profession.

A friend of mine secured his first job as a newspaper reporter through the Society of Professional Journalists. He contacted the local chapter president and that president was able to put him in contact with a newspaper that was looking to fill a reporter position. Another friend of mine has a son who recently graduated from vocational school in which he earned an electrician's degree. That man got his job by contacting the local electrician's union. They were able to refer him to two different employers that were hiring electricians.

7) **"Now Hiring" posters/"Help Wanted" signs.** As I write this book, the economy in the U.S. is very strong and there are many job openings. When the economy is strong like this, you'll note that many, many businesses have "Now Hiring" or "Help Wanted" signs posted on their premises. If you think that any of these businesses would be a good place to work, I suggest that you visit the location and ask to speak to the manager or to complete an application. Are there any businesses you frequent that seem like they would be great places to work? If so, you may want to ask who does the hiring there and then introduce yourself. It should be noted that this is a great way to get seasonal jobs if you are looking to make extra cash. (i.e.-The holiday season.)

Using the Internet to Find Your Dream Job

It shouldn't surprise you to find out that the internet provides a great way to help you find and get your dream job. On the other hand, internet information is so readily available and the fact that a person can complete a job application in the comfort of his own living room (maybe even wearing pajamas), often leads to many more applications for the same job. Here are some ways you can use the internet to get your dream job:

1) **Monitor job openings directly on a company's web site.** I detailed this in the previous section. A company's web site often offers a great way to find out if they have any current openings.

2) **Research your desired company.** In the "old days", people who were interested to work for a specific company were encouraged to get their hands on the company's annual report or the company's promotional literature. This information would hopefully provide enough information about the company so that the job applicant could refer to some of this information in his cover letter. Now, it is extremely easy to learn about any company you might be interested. You can simply go to their web site, where you can get lots of information about the products they sell or the services they offer. If

you're smart, you'll use some of the information you glean from the web site in your cover letter to the company (along with your resume, of course.)

3)   **Find great companies to work for.** There's no lack of "great companies to work for" information on the internet. If you are not totally sure of what company you want to work for, but you know that you just want to work for a good company, the internet is full of articles on which companies are great to work for. If you have a particular area or region in mind, you can easily fine-tune your search. i.e.-Great companies to work for in Boston area.

4)   **Professional associations, organizations.** Again, I covered some of this in the previous section, but the internet provides a great way for you to find out the names and contact information of professional organizations, associations, unions, fraternities, etc. Many of these organizations post their newsletters online or allow you to get free emailed copies of their newsletter. Newsletters provide another great way for you to learn about the industry you are interested in. Some of them even contain job postings.

5)   **Job sites.** There are many job search sites on the internet. Many employers use these sites to post job openings and secure applications. If you're looking for a job, it is important to remember that many companies use only one or two sites to post their job openings and just because you don't find an opening for a company on one site doesn't mean that it will not be posted on another site. I suggest that you start out by browsing multiple job sites and then as you become more familiar with the sites, you'll be able to determine which sites you feel most comfortable with, which sites offer the most jobs in your field, etc.

Some of the most popular job sites currently include: Indeed, Monster, Glassdoor, ZipRecruiter, and CareerBuilder. I encourage you to browse each of these sites a number of times and then if you want to eliminate some of them from you rostrum, you can do so after you determine which ones are most likely to be effective for your search.

How to Find Jobs that Aren't Advertised.

Nearly half of all available job openings are never advertised, so you'll need to keep this in mind as you do your search. Some companies don't advertise job openings because of the cost involved. Others don't advertise because they're interested to hire from within. And some companies don't want to advertise because they don't want to sort through the multitude of applications they might receive through advertising an opening.

Its important to note that nearly half of all jobs are not advertised. As someone who is looking for a job, this means that you'll have to find ways to access these unadvertised jobs.

The most popular means of finding unadvertised jobs is through some sort of networking. Social networks such as Facebook and Twitter can be effective in helping you find these jobs. In order to do that however, you'll probably need to have an established presence on these sites. Someone who has 750 to 1000 Facebook or Twitter followers is certainly likely to be more successful than someone who has a couple dozen followers. And if you have a limited number of followers on your social media platforms, it's going to be difficult for you to gain a larger number of followers in a short time. So, if you have a solid presence on Facebook or Twitter, I'd suggest that you consider them as a possible source for information or referrals in your job search.

Even if you don't have much of a presence on Facebook or Twitter, I strongly suggest that you establish a presence on LinkedIn, which is primarily a business site that has groups for specific industries. For example, if you are an engineer, LinkedIn has a group specifically for engineers. If you are a marketeer, LinkedIn has specific groups for marketing professionals. These groups include not only people looking for jobs, but employers who are looking to hire people and recruiters who are looking to place people.

Another benefit to LinkedIn is that it offers you the opportunity to apply for multiple jobs in just a short amount of time. You'll save time by not having to write cover letters. You'll also save time by not having to fill out some of the tedious applications which are required on some of the job search or individual company sites. As a matter of fact, you might be able to apply for up to 20 jobs in just 30 minutes. (It might take you 30 minutes to apply for just one job on an individual company site or one of the internet job search sites.) Depending on what kind of job you're looking for, you should remember that looking for jobs can sometimes be a numbers game. The more jobs you apply for, the better chance you have of getting a job. LinkedIn is a great medium for this approach and I encourage you to use it as such.

And, as discussed before, don't ignore other possible sources for unadvertised job openings. This includes alumni associations or school career centers and professional associations or organizations. And if you have established a target company or companies, don't hesitate to contact them even if they are not advertising any openings. A company that has no openings today may be only a day away from having an opening…or, even better, they may have an opening that they haven't advertised yet.

One other piece of advice as you begin your job hunt. Try not to focus on the rejections or the non-responses that you receive. As mentioned above, job hunting is often a numbers game and you're more likely to get an interview or a job by applying for many jobs than you are if you apply for just a few jobs. I had a friend who, when he looked for a job, would send out one resume at a time, waiting to receive a response from that application before he sent out another application. When he finally admitted that his process didn't make sense, he sent out multiple applications at the same time, realizing that he could never control whether a prospective employer was interested in him or not.

Job Search

My friend finally realized that it only takes one yes to make up for all the rejections and non-responses. He realized that he couldn't control the results, but he could control the process. He resolved to apply for at least 10 jobs per day until he had an acceptable job offer. It ends up that he had three invitations to interview within a week. And he finally had to choose between two attractive offers. That was a nice problem to have and he admitted later that once he had discovered the process he needed to use to get a job, the results followed…quickly.

Chapter 2—A Resume to Beat Them All

Creating a Killer Resume.

If you're going to have a chance to get your dream job, your first goal should be to get your "foot in the door". If you can't get an interview, you won't have a chance to get the job you want. A top-notch resume will be an extremely important tool for you to use in securing interviews.

In developing a resume, it's important to remember that the company or person you're sending your resume to will most likely be receiving lots of applications for the same job and, in order for you to have a chance, your resume will have to make you stand out among other applicants.

With this in mind, here are some simple steps you can use to create a killer resume:

1)   Review resume samples. Before you establish your own resume, it will be beneficial for you to know what other resumes look like. You'll find resume samples all over the internet, including resume samples that are categorized according to specific professions, such as advertising, marketing, sales, accounting, nursing, secretarial, janitorial…just about any profession you can imagine. When you review these resume samples, you should place yourself in the shoes of the person who is doing the hiring and decide which resume formats would appeal to you if you were in the hiring position. And please note that resumes are often catered to specific professions. For example, a resume for an advertising position is likely to be set up differently than a resume for an accounting position. Once you have a feel for what kind of resume you want to develop, you should…

2)   Find a resume template. A template provides a cookie-cutter approach for you to use in developing your resume. It provides a starting point for you to use in setting up your resume. Although you will most likely be modifying or tweaking your resume for each job you apply for, the resume template will provide you with a structure to use in making sure that you have included all pertinent information on the resume. There are tons of different free resume templates on the internet, including some different options from Microsoft Word. I suggest that you review some different templates and find one that fits your personality and also the type of job for which you are applying. Again, the profession you are applying for may determine how creative you will want to be with your resume design. For example, a person who is applying for an advertising or graphic arts position may well be expected to have a more visually appealing resume than a person who is applying for an accounting or a janitorial position. If you're looking for an internet site that shows a nice variety of sample resumes for specific professions, I suggest myperfectresume.com, where they have resume examples for lots of different professions, ranging from social services to transportation to restaurant and hotel hospitality to retail to information technology…just about any professional category you can imagine. This site also offers some free templates for you to use in developing your resume.

3) **Determine a font.** After you've determined the template you're going to use for your resume, you should determine a font to use for the resume. For those of you who are not familiar with what a font is, it is simply the typestyle you will use for the words in your resume. If you are typing your resume in a Microsoft Word document, you will be able to choose what font you want to use. In determining a font for your resume, again please keep the person who is doing the hiring in mind. I always suggest that people use simple, basic fonts for their resumes, making the resume as easy to read as possible. You won't want to use a fancy typestyle on your resume; that's not an effective way to stand out among other applicants.

4)   Add your contact information. Obviously, you'll want to list all of your contact information on your resume, including your phone number(s), your email address, and at least the city and state where you live. Some applicants will choose to list their entire address; others do not. Either way, the goal is for the company or person doing the hiring to be able to contact you easily. If you have multiple phone numbers, I suggest that you give them the number that you will answer all the time. The same goes for email addresses. If you have multiple email addresses, you need to make sure that you give them you should give them only your preferred email address. And then make sure you are checking your phone and email messages daily. I had a young man I was mentoring who did not check his email messages every day and, as a result, he missed an invitation to interview for a job he had applied for. If you're applying for jobs, it's important that you are accessible for prospective employers.

5)   Write your objective. At or near the top of every resume, you should write your objective in applying for the job. This is a part of a resume which is often customized, based on the specifics of the job you're applying for. With one or two sentences, you'll list why you are applying for the position. For example, a young woman who was applying for a restaurant chain marketing position listed her objectives as follows: "I am looking to meld my three years of marketing experience with my two years of working for a franchised printing chain in a hospitality-oriented industry." As another example, a man looking for a job as a bookseller with Barnes & Noble listed his career objectives as follows: "I have been a loyal and frequent Barnes & Noble customer for years. As an avid reader, I am knowledgeable in many book genres, and I am interested to use my passion for and my knowledge of books into a career as a bookseller." With your objective, you will be telling the hirer why you are applying for the position and also, hopefully, why you are a good fit to be hired for that position.

6) **List important and relevant accomplishments.** With any resume, it will be important for you to list any information that will be relevant to the job you are applying for. This information should be placed in order of relevance to the open position. Again, referring back to the young woman who was applying for a chain restaurant marketing position, the fact that she had three years marketing experience was obviously relevant to the position she was applying for. Along the same lines, since that restaurant chain was a chain that had multiple franchised locations, she mentioned that she had experience working with a franchised chain. Even though her experience was with a franchised print shop chain instead of a restaurant chain, she realized that her experience in working with franchisees of any sort might well be beneficial or applicable to in the position she was applying for.

7) **Pay attention to the job description and use keywords from this description in your resume.** There are a couple of reasons why you need to refer to keywords in the job description for any job you are applying for. First, you may or may not be aware that some companies use software bots or software programs to pre-screen applications. These bots or software programs are designed to search for keywords that apply to the open job position. These bots are used to filter out resumes that may not pertain specifically to the job opening that was advertised. Some companies are inundated with resumes for job openings and the use of a software program offers the company a way to reduce the amount of resumes that are even seen by the person that is doing the hiring. As these bots are designed to search out key words that are often included in the job description, it will be important for you to place some of these keywords in your resume. Second, if the company or person doing the hiring has listed specific traits or things they are looking for from an applicant and these things are applicable to you, then you should make sure to reinforce these keywords in telling the prospective employer why you would be well-suited for the job. For example, if the job posting says that the employer is looking for a "self-motivated individual" you might mention in your resume that although you can take direction very well,

you are also self-motivated to the point where you can take a project and run with it. In using some of the job descriptions keywords, you'll not only be showing them that you read their posting, but, more importantly, that you are the right person for the job.

8) Optimize and organize information. I always tell job applicants to limit their resumes to two pages maximum; possibly one page, depending on the job they are applying for. In organizing your information, it's important that you place the most pertinent information near the top of the resume. For example, if a person has been working for 20 years and they graduated from college 20 years ago, their educational background is probably going to be a lot less pertinent than their work experience. Thus, education information should appear lower in the resume. Or, if a person is applying for a restaurant marketing job, and they have previously had a restaurant marketing job with another company even though that may not have been their most recent job, it might be appropriate to list that restaurant experience nearer to the top of the resume than the non-restaurant related job experience.

How to Tailor Your Resume to a Specific Job.

If you want to enhance the chances to get an interview for the jobs you're applying for, you're almost certainly going to have to tailor your resume to the specific job you're applying for. If you don't do that, the company or person who is hiring is likely to presume that you aren't very interested in their job opening and you're likely to fall toward the bottom of the resume pile.

Once you have all of the basic information on your resume template form, it will be much easier to adapt this information to fit any job you are applying for.

There are some simple ways you can customize your resume to fit the job you are applying for:

Job Search

1) Identify the things that are important to the employer. You can do this by reading the job description. What things does the employer say they are looking for in an employee? What qualities or traits appear near the top of the ad? These are likely to be more important than qualities or traits that appear near the bottom of the ad. Does the job post mention anything a number of times or repetitively? If so, this is probably something that is particularly important to the employer.

2) Once you've identified the things that appear to be important to the employer in the job listing, you should then match these things with the various things listed on your resume. For example, if the job post emphasizes that they want to hire someone who has leadership abilities, you should find experiences in your background in which you had to lead others. Even if you haven't previously mentioned leadership on your resume, you should review your past experiences to see if you had any leadership roles and then, if so, add those experiences to your tailored resume. Or maybe the employer is looking to hire someone who is a good multi-tasker. Do you have any examples to add to your resume that show that you are a capable multi-tasker? If so, please emphasize this on your resume. It will not be enough to just list that you are good at multi-tasking on your resume. Most employers will be able to see through this. You should give specific examples of your multi-tasking experience. In tailoring your resume, it will behoove you to be as specific as possible. If you're interviewing for a sales position and you've had previous success in a sales position, you could mention that sales percentage increase you had in that previous position. If you are interviewing for a management position, you could mention that you managed a staff of 14 people in your previous job and/or that you hired and trained four new employees in that position. The more specific you can be, the more believable you'll be with the examples you're giving.

3) Add/remove/reorder/modify. In tailoring your resume to a specific job, it is important that you remain flexible in adapting your resume. Don't hesitate to move elements of your resume around, including the order of the items shown. If something from your resume is not at all pertinent with this job, don't hesitate to remove it. And if, based on the description in the job post, you find any other parcels from your background that might help you get an interview, you should add those items to your resume. Again, you don't want your resume to become too long, so if you are adding some parcels, you might delete others. If you can't fit all the information that you want in the resume itself, you might consider placing any pertinent extra information in your cover letter.

4) Use the tailored resume to prepare for your interview. If you're fortunate enough to secure an interview based on your tailored resume, you'll be able to use that information to determine talking points or points of emphasis in your interview. For example, if the person interviewing you asks you to tell them about yourself or to tell you why you are interested in their job, you will be able to use those talking points to answer those questions, knowing full well what is important to them in their search for an employee. Instead of rambling on about things that may not be important to them, you should be able to pinpoint the areas they are interested in. That should enhance your chances for success in any interview.

How to Write Great Cover Letters.

Whenever you get the opportunity, you should write a cover letter to accompany your resume. Cover letters will allow you a chance to expand and go beyond your resume. The goal of a cover letter should be to get the person reading it to want to review your resume and hopefully to get a quick glimpse as to why you are a good candidate for the open position. Here are some random tips, techniques, and thoughts for writing an effective cover letter. Although not all of these tips may apply to your particular cover letter, these ideas will give you some things to consider in drafting your letter.

1) **Try to limit your cover letter to one page.** Certainly, never more than two pages.

2) **If possible, address the cover letter to the attention of the person who Is doing the hiring.** If you do this, make sure you have the correct spelling of the person whose name you are using. You can decide whether you want to use a more formal reference such as Ms. or Mr. I generally prefer less casual, such as first names. However, if you are using a first name, you should probably do some research as to what first name the person goes by. For example, does someone named Charles go by Charles, Charlie, Chaz, or Chuck? Does James go by James, Jim, or Jimmy? If you are going to use a first name, I suggest you make sure of their name preference. If you're not sure of the name the hirer goes by, a simple phone call to the receptionist at the company should provide the necessary information. Simply tell them that you want to send correspondence to this person and find out what their name preference is.

3) **Your tone in a cover letter should be conversational instead of formal.** Whereas your resume should be formal, your cover letter should be much less formal. Cover letters offer you the opportunity to "write between the lines", telling the reader who are you as a person, telling them why you are interested in the job they are offering, and telling them why you are a good fit for that job. When you are writing your cover letters, you should use a conversational tone. In other words, write it as you would say it, as if you are having a conversation with the person who is reading it. In doing this, you'll be able to show your prospective employer that you are much more than just a formal list of resume credentials.

4) **With your cover letter, you'll need to do more than to simply highlight or rehash the information that you included on your accompanying resume.**

5) Use your cover letter as a chance to expand upon one or some of the talking points in your resume. Expand upon why you are the right person for the job, maybe highlighting in further detail some of your experiences or accomplishments. For example, if the company's job description states that it is important for the applicant to be a self-starter, you should highlight the fact that you work well with or without supervision and that you can take a project from start to finish without a lot of supervision. If the company is looking for someone who can multi-task and work on multiple projects at the same time, you should highlight any past experience you've had with that. Here's an excerpt from one of my clients, who was applying for a public relations job which required attention to multiple projects at the same time: "Your job description notes that this position will require the ability to multi-task. As a public relations associate for IDQ, I coordinated many projects at the same time, including the company's milk carton boat race sponsorship, the company's systemwide support of the National Kidney Foundation, the company's Run, Hit, and Throw youth baseball competition, and the coordination of press conferences announcing the introduction of the company's new institutional foods program. All were major public relations programs that I handled successfully." As you'll note by this excerpt, the applicant certainly provided proof that they could handle multiple projects concurrently. And I like that fact that they were very specific in detailing those projects. Much better than just saying "I'm able to multi-task" and leaving it at that.

6) If possible, your opening line should be one that will grab the attention of the reader. Although it's important to grab the reader's attention, I wouldn't do so at the risk of being corny or hokey. You might incorporate your experience, your passion, or your past accomplishments into the opening sentence. For example, here's the opening lines of a cover letter that someone wrote with an application for a Barnes & Noble bookseller job: "Over the years, I've spent a lot of time in your Barnes & Noble bookstore. I'm an avid reader and I love the Barnes & Noble concept. With this passion and knowledge of books and with my penchant for great customer service, I feel like I'll be a great fit for your opening for a bookseller." With these opening lines, you'll note that the applicant mentions the job he is applying for, he compliments the company, he explains how he will fit within that company with his passion for books, and he also details that he is good at customer service. In just three sentences, he's given the reader some reasons why he should be near the top of the resume pile.

If you can't think of anything in particular to grab the reader, then I suggest that you go with something more generic, such as, "I'm excited to apply for your marketing associate position at ABC Company. I've read some articles regarding your company and visited your company web site and, with my experience and enthusiasm, I think I can become a valuable asset there."

7) **As you'll note by the previous sentence, the applicant is outlining what he can do for the company instead of what the company can do for him.** You should avoid mentioning what the company can do for you, as the person who is hiring already knows what the company can do for you.

8) **In any cover letter, you should outline the things you can "bring to the party".** How can you become an asset to the company that is hiring. If you have experiences, expertise, or knowledge that will allow you to become an asset there, you should mention those things in your cover letter. Even if you don't have much experience to bring to the table, you can certainly mention less tangent things such as energy, enthusiasm, passion, the willingness to learn, the willingness to work hard, etc.

9) **If you have numbers to prove your case, use them.** For example, a friend of mine who was applying for a sales job listed numbers from his previous sales job in which he was the top salesperson from a salesforce of 9. His sales accounted for 36% of company sales, he brought in 20% of the company's new customers, and he won Salesperson of the Year each of the three years he was there. Another example, for someone who was applying for a supervisory position in which the person who be responsible for hiring, training, and managing a staff of about 10 people, the applicant mentioned that she had successfully hired and trained a department of seven accountants or accounting assistants, and her department had the lowest turnover rate of any department within the company.

10) Testimonials. If you have any testimonials or testaments to your abilities or talents, a cover letter is a good place to use them. Going back to the aforementioned accounting supervisor, she used the following testimonial in her cover letter. "One of the employees I hired and trained, told me that I was the fourth boss she had and that I was the first boss who had taken the time with her to make her a valuable employee. She later became our department's employee of the year and she later told me that the help I had given her had a major impact on her career." Again, these testimonials are things that you normally would not include in a resume, however they work well in cover letters and they might well help differentiate you from other applicants and get you to the top of the resume pile.

11) Don't be afraid to pat yourself on the back. A cover letter is a good place to trumpet your previous achievements or accomplishments. Remember, if you don't toot your own horn during the interview process, no one else is going to do that for you.

12) Finish strong. Your final sentence or final paragraph of your resume will be your last shot at making an impression with the reader. Make sure you finish strong, possible reiterating why you would like to work for the company, what you can bring to the table, or why you would be a good fit. And again, if you don't have any tangible assets, maybe because you're applying for your first job or you're new to the workforce, you can always promise that you are willing to learn or to work hard to become a valued asset of the company.

13) **Edit and review.** It almost goes without saying that you need to check your cover letter (and resume) for spelling, grammar, and punctuation errors. I know people who hire who will discard perfectly good candidates due to spelling or grammar errors, even if spelling and grammar are unrelated to the job opening. Some people view these areas as carelessness, lack of attention to detail, etc. So, I'd recommend that you use spell-check to check your content. Also, if you know people who can read your resume and cover letter to then provide feedback before it goes to the prospective employer, you should ask for their assistance.

Again, the goal of any cover letter is to get the reader to read the accompanying resume. The goal of a resume is to get you an interview. The goal of both the cover letter and the resume are to separate you from all of the other applicants for the same opening. Keep this in mind when writing your cover letter. If it is so blah that it doesn't make an impression, you probably won't get an interview.

Chapter 3 - Get Ahead with an Online Portfolio

If you want to enhance your chances to get jobs or projects, you should consider having an online presence, if you don't already have one. If you can build your own personal brand online, you'll be able to supplement any resume or cover letter you send out. And you can do so very economically, even for free.

Before we delve deeper into what you can do to establish an online presence that will help you get the job of your dreams, let's briefly discuss the online presence you already have, especially in regards to social media.

Before you embark upon your job search, I strongly suggest that you review your social media presence and make sure none of that image will impact your ability to get a job. It's no secret that many employers will look you up on social media before extending a job offer. I've had job search clients who have lost job opportunities because of their online presence. One of my clients was a recent college grad whose Facebook page was full of party photos, some of which showed him in what looked to be a drunken state. Another of my clients had a Facebook page which was riddled by inappropriate language; another had a page which was laced with political rants. Certainly, these items should have been cleaned up before they embarked on their job search. In searching for a job, you should presume that your prospective employer will check to see what kind of an online presence you have, including platforms such as Facebook, Instagram, Twitter, etc.

Also, they will probably do a Google search on you to see if there are any stories or blurbs about you on the internet. There may be things about you on the internet that you can't delete or clean up. But you should at least know what information about you is readily available on the internet and then if any of that information is negative, you should probably have an explanation for that information, as you may be asked about it by a prospective employer. I had a young client who was arrested for breaking and entering into a golf clubhouse when he was 17. His name appeared in the small town newspaper and that information remains on the internet and is something that still haunts him even years later. He has an unusual name, so there is no doubt that he was involved in the crime. So, now he is prepared to expound on this incident if asked about it by prospective employers. Honesty is his best policy in explaining that it was a dumb adolescent mistake that he deeply regrets and will not repeat.

So, the bottom line is that before you start your job search, make sure you take a look at your social media presence. Look at it through the eyes of a prospective employer and make sure that it's not going to impact you negatively. If so, correct whatever you can correct and be prepared to explain whatever you can't correct.

Tips for Building an Online Portfolio That Gets You Hired.

Now that you've reviewed and filtered the online presence you already have, you can move forward and establish a presence that will assist you in your job search efforts. Depending on your profession or the job you are looking to secure, you'll have to figure out whether you want to have a graphic presence, a written presence, or both. If you are a commercial artist, a photographer, a graphic designer, a cake decorator, an event planner, those are professions or vocations that are conducive toward a visual presence on the internet. If you are a freelance writer, a household budgeting expert, or a relationship counselor, those professions are conducive to a written presence on the internet, possibly a blog presence. LinkedIn is a business and employment-oriented platform that is probably the most popular means to establish an online professional presence. We'll discuss that platform specifically later in the chapter. But for now, I'd like to inform you about other possible ways you can create an online professional presence or brand.

Job Search

1) **Web site.** These days, setting up a simple web site is quite easy. You don't need to be a coder and you should be able to set it up yourself if you are even a bit tech savvy. Sites such as Squarespace, Wix, HostGator, and GoDaddy are all web site hosts that have inexpensive site hosting that range in price from free to $15 per month, depending on the features you want. All of these sites are geared toward consumers who want to set up simple web sites and they offer simple instructions on how to do so. In having your own personal web site, you can promote some of your skills. My daughter-in-law is a wedding planner and she has a simple web site which contains photos of the different weddings she has planned over the years. This web site is vital to her business and she has obtained numerous gigs as a result of the web site. I have a client who is a graphic artist who also has his own site. On the site, he has posted samples of some of the projects he's done and he uses the site as a portfolio for his talents and abilities. Although he is a freelancer now, he previously used a similar web site to get his job as a corporate artist.

If any of your areas of expertise are conducive to visual representation, I suggest you consider creating your own web site to promote and display your talents. In doing so, you should also make sure you have an About You section in which you tell a bit about yourself. You can use this page as an extension of your resume, although it should be a lot less formal and more conversational. You can convey as much information as you'd like, but you should remember that your viewers will be typical web browsers who will spend a minimal amount of time on each page. So, there's no need to write a book about yourself for this section of the web site.

2) **Blogs.** Maybe your area of expertise is more verbal than graphic. If so, you might consider creating a blog to promote yourself. Again, there are many inexpensive blog platforms available to you, including Wix, Squarespace, and WordPress. Monthly hosting charges are very nominal, and this a great way to advertise your talents and expertise. As an example, I have a friend of mine who makes her living as a professional dog trainer. She writes a monthly blog which includes stories and tips about dog training. With her blog, she has established herself as an expert in the field. You can do the same with your blog. Another friend of mine is a freelance writer who has samples of about 25 different pieces she has written on her blog site. So, in searching for a job, you can direct a prospective employer to your blog site and they'll be able to spend as much time there as they would like in reading your blogs.

If you are not a proficient writer by trade, that shouldn't necessarily discourage you from having a blog, as you can hire freelance writers who can do that for you, often inexpensively. Upwork is a freelance platform on which you can have blogs written anywhere from $15 to $50 per blog. In hiring a freelancer, you should remember that they can only be as good as the information you give them, so be prepared to furnish them with an outline of the information you want contained in the blog.

3) **YouTube**. Maybe your talent or area of expertise is better shown in video format. If so, you should consider posting some short video clips on YouTube. I have quite a few clients who have established themselves as experts in their fields by posting video tutorials on YouTube. I know two people who are information technology gurus who post video clips regarding how to solve various computer problems for people who are not tech-oriented. The guy who does my small engine repair (lawnmower, vacuum cleaner) has a series of video tutorials on Facebook, as does my appliance repairman. With these tutorials, it should be pointed out that they are not necessarily professionally done, as a television infomercial would be. These tutorials are simply done, by one person, no production crew. The information provided is much more important than the production quality and these short videos establish the creators as experts in their field. You can do the same thing in establishing yourself as an expert in your field and this can definitely help as you search for a job.

When a prospective employer is searching job candidates, you'll be able to vault to the top of the resume pile if you can show them that you are an expert in your field or good at what you do. As you may find out in your own job search, getting the job of your dreams often involves a lot more than just having a resume and a cover letter. You'll want to make sure that you have a professional presence on the internet.

The Lowdown on Creating an Irresistible LinkedIn Profile.

If you're looking to find a job or if you're looking to increase your professional visibility or establish your professional brand, using LinkedIn is a "must". LinkedIn is the largest online professional networking site. It is a platform that many employers and recruiters use in securing job candidates. A platform that is geared toward professionals, LinkedIn offers professionals the opportunity to network, to search job openings or job candidates, and for members to showcase their professional abilities, talents, accomplishments, and achievements.

I've compiled some simple tips and techniques which you can use to establish a top-notch presence on LinkedIn. This information should be beneficial to you as you create or enhance your LinkedIn profile.

1) **The more complete, the better**. In establishing your LinkedIn profile, you'll want to make sure that you complete every section of the profile. A prospective employer is likely to frown upon a candidate who does not have a complete profile. And in completing your profile, please make sure you tell people what your skills are and where you've worked.

2) **Use a conversational, passionate, optimistic tone**. With the information you include in your LinkedIn profile, you should always use a conversational, somewhat casual tone. Hopefully, you'll be able to convey some of your personality with your LinkedIn profile.

Job Search

Remember that any prospective employer will be looking at numerous profiles and you'll want to make sure that this person gets a quick feel for your personality as they read your profile. Always use the first person (I or me) when referring to yourself. And be sure to show your enthusiasm or passion toward what you do or what you want to do. For example, with my friend who was seeking a bookselling job, he included his passion in his profile: "I love books. I love reading them, I love discussing them, I love sharing them with others, and I'm sure I'll love selling them." With just this short statement, the reader understands quickly that this person is a booklover. His passion shows immediately.

3) Show numbers if you have them. Besides showing passion, show numbers. Prospective employers often like numbers, something tangible to rate your abilities. If you are a graphic artist, you might mention that you've done over 400 projects for over 70 different clients. And that your retention rate for your customers is over 95%. If you're in the advertising business, you might mention that one of the ad campaigns you designed produced a 300% sales increase when the goal had been a 25% increase. Anything you can do to correlate tangible numbers with your accomplishments will make you look better in the eyes of anyone who might be interested in hiring you.

4) Use a great photo of yourself. Although this might seem obvious, some people make the mistake of not posting a good photo in conjunction with their profile. In your photo, you should be dressed appropriately for your position or the position your interested in. And, if you can, it will be good if you can use a photo which shows you in action. For example, if you have guest speaking experience and you have a photo of you talking to an audience, that may well be preferable to just a plain headshot. Or if you are a corporate attorney, you might post a photo of you meeting with a client or inside a courtroom.

5) **Write an attention-grabbing headline.** Again, remembering that any prospective employer will be looking at multiple profiles, it will be important for you to grab the viewer's attention as soon as possible, hopefully with an attention-grabbing headline. As an example, a friend of mine who is a freelance writer who offers quick turnaround has used a "Fastest Pen in the West" headline for her profile. Anything you can do to separate yourself from other candidates will give you a better chance to get the job you're looking for.

6) **Add multi-media to your profile.** LinkedIn profiles offer you the opportunity to "show and tell" your talents, abilities, experiences, and achievements. Any samples you can show to tell prospective employers why you are the person for the job or why you are an expert in your field will increase your chances in getting the job of your dreams. And, as we all know, people love visual accompaniments. With this in mind, you should see if you can enhance your LinkedIn profile by adding accompaniments such as photos, video clips, blogs, or slideshows. Again, these should all be related to your professional career, with the goal of showcasing your talents or expertise. In most instances, these visual aides should be placed in the summary area of your profile.

You can also enhance your profile by providing links to any articles about you or photos of you on the internet, even if it's just a mention for a professional achievement. If you have been an employee for a company that is not well-known, you might also provide a link to that company's web site, so the prospective employer can get an idea of who you worked for. In providing links to your professional achievements or your previous places of employment, you'll also be directing any searches that prospective employers might be doing on you.

7) **Connections.** With your LinkedIn profile, you should also know that it will be important for you to have a significant number of connections. As a rule of thumb, you should try to have at least 50 connections. Anything less than that may be a red flag to prospective

employers who may think you're a hermit, you're anti-social or simply not interested in connecting with others, you're not technology- or social media-oriented, or you're just not a viable candidate. In establishing connections, you should remember that it's not a contest to see who has the most connections, however you want to at least have enough connections to establish your credibility. Don't add people you don't know. If you have enough people who are rejecting your connection requests because they say they don't know you, LinkedIn reserves the right to shut down your profile.

8) **Keep your job search confidential.** If you have a current job, you might not want your current employer to know that you're looking to find another job. If this is the case, you can use the LinkedIn privacy settings to make sure that your current employer doesn't know that you are looking to find another job.

9) **Make sure people know how to find you.** Just a quick reminder to make sure that your resume includes your contact information. (email address, Twitter handle, blog, etc.—someplace you check for messages, at least on a daily basis.) You'd be surprised how many people forget to include this simple and pertinent information on their resumes.

10) **Request recommendations**. It will be important for you to have recommendations from current and former business associates. Don't be shy in asking your contacts to provide testimonials. And if you have any particular area or subject for which you'd like them to provide the testimonial, don't hesitate to tell them what subject you'd like them to broach. And, remember, you can control/select the recommendations you show on your profile. So, you can use these recommendations to show whatever areas of strength or expertise your interested in, and you can change these on an on-going basis as you adjust your preferences.

11) Groups. One of the best features of LinkedIn is that it has LinkedIn Groups that can be invaluable in helping you to secure a job within your industry. By joining groups which are related to your industry or profession, you'll be able to show that you are involved and engaged in that industry and you'll be able to connect to people who have access to information about job openings, industry trends or talking points, etc. These LinkedIn groups offer ongoing, online network opportunities which you can utilize in your job search.

12) Always include current job listing, even if unemployed. As most prospective employers use only the current title box on LinkedIn to look for candidates, it's important that you list a current position in the experience section of your profile. If you're unemployed, you should simply list your most recent position or the position or field you're looking for and then follow that with a further title description in the company name box. As an example, you can list the following: Graduating student/marketing major. List that in the current job title box. And then in the company name box, list "In transition" or "Seeking career opportunities". Either way, it's important to make sure you don't leave the current job box empty, so employers who are searching only the current title box section will be able to access your profile.

How a Blog Can Boost Your Career.

Earlier in this chapter, I mentioned that having a blog can be an excellent means of placing you above the clutter of candidates in your efforts to find a job. I'll now expound upon why a blog can be an important tool in helping you get that job you want to get.

Blogs can be used to complement your resume. Although a resume outlines your previous work and education experiences, a blog can be used to expand on that. As resumes are somewhat restrictive in the amount of information they can contain, blogs allow you to showcase your knowledge and expertise. They can provide prospective employers with a better look into who you are and what your talents and abilities are.

Blogs allow you to establish yourself as an expert or leader in your field. They also provide an excellent means for you to build and promote your personal brand. In having a blog, you'll also establish that fact that you have a digital footprint—you're internet and social media savvy and you know how to use technology to promote yourself and to reach others. A blog will also show that you have passion and pride in your career or profession.

As resumes and cover letters are traditionally restricted in length to two pages or less, blogs offer a great way for you to expound on your experience and convey who you are to prospective employers. Employers and recruiters are always looking for ways to differentiate job candidates from each other.

In establishing a blog, I suggest that you have at least three or four blogs available for reading immediately after you start your blogs. One blog is not enough to give the reader an idea as to your areas of expertise. You'll want at least a few blogs to retain the reader. And then after your initial postings, I would recommend that you add a new blog at least once a month, hopefully at the same time each month. Ideally, you will have a registration mechanism on your blog site that allows you to send them notifications as to when your blogs are available on your hosting site. An average blog length goes from 500 to 1000 words, although you can certainly use any length for your blogs. Again, if you are not a proficient writer, but have valuable information to disseminate, you can always hire a freelance writer to write your blogs for you. This can be done inexpensively. If you're hiring a freelancer to write your blog, you should remember that a freelancer is only as good as the information you provide to him or her.

Six Fabulous Tools to Help You Put Together Your Online Portfolio.

Job Search

Here are some additional tools for you to use in developing your online portfolio. We've mentioned some of these tools before; others may be new to you.

1) **LinkedIn.** We've already discussed this at length, however I want to mention it again, because it's a vital tool for you to use in establishing your online portfolio. You can add visuals, videos, audios, and files. And it's free.

2) **Vizualize.me.** A solid platform that allows you to choose from a multitude of different themes and styles to chronicle your career in a visual format. Connects to LinkedIn.

3) **Personal web sites.** Lots of web site concepts to choose from, including Weebly, Wix, Squarespace, GoDaddy, and HostGator. These sites, which are either free or available at a nominal price, all allow professionals to build their own personal sites quickly and easily. Most of these concepts have many different stock templates and styles for you to choose from in designing a site that fits you, your personality, and your experience.

4) **About.me.** This site offers a simple way for anyone to build a landing page that includes images and brief text.

5) **Blog sites.** WordPress, Squarespace, and Wix are among sites that special in personal blog hosting. All offer different design templates for you to choose from.

6) **PortfolioBox.** This is a portfolio design platform that works particularly well for professional people who have a lot of visual items to display. This includes photographers, graphic designers, and artists, who can show lots of samples of their works on the platform.

Job Search

Thousands of themes to choose from. Optimized for smartphone and tablet viewing. Also great for other business professional who have a lot of visual to show.

As you can see, there are many different tools and platforms available for you to establish an online professional presence that supplements your resume. If you want to get to the top of the pack as a job candidate, the best way to ensure that will be to establish an impressive online presence, where you can convey your talents and abilities to a prospective employer who is looking to find the difference between all job candidates.

Chapter 4—Networking for Success

Before I fully understood the concept of networking, I was reluctant to do it. I always had the idea that if I networked, I would come across as being self-serving, pushy, and maybe even annoying. But then a friend of mine put networking into a different perspective for me, telling me that networking is simply the concept of keeping my eyes open and building better relationship whenever possible, with the people I know and also with people I don't know. Hands down, networking can be one of the most effective means of getting a job.

The fundamentals of networking. Just as the mantra of successful real estate is "location, location, location", the mantra of successful networking is "connect, connect, connect". You may not realize it, but you already have your own network. Whether it is your business associates, your old high school and college friends, the parents of your kids' schoolmates, people who are in your volunteer group, or the people you play pickup basketball with, all of these people are people who could help you get your next job.

It's important to remember a couple of things in regards to networking. First of all, you should know that people prefer to do business with people they have some kind of connection to. Resumes and cover letters are important, however they're often too impersonal to get someone to hire you. Second, as we've mentioned before, most job listings get lots of applicants. With this in mind, you'll need a point of difference that can place you above the other people applying for the same job. Finally, you should note that many jobs are not advertised. Networking can result in job leads that you will not get through regular job search channels. Maybe these jobs will never be advertised or maybe they've yet to be advertised and you'll get a jump on the job posting.

Before you begin networking, you should make a list of the people in your network. In doing this, you'll surely find that this list is much larger than you thought it would be. In listing your contacts, you should include family, friends, neighbors, co-workers and colleagues, high school and college schoolmates, social media contacts, email contacts, and casual acquaintances. And don't forget other people you do business with on a regular basis, including your doctor, your dentist, your dry cleaner, your pharmacist, your yoga instructor, your landlord, your accountant, etc. And likewise, don't forget other people you come into contact with on a regular basis, including fellow civic members, health club members, volunteer group members, church members, etc.

Always remember that each member of a network has the capability to provide invaluable information about a job opening or they may know someone who can help. Don't ignore anyone. A client of mine, who is a restaurant marketing executive, first found out about the opening for the job he now has through his dry cleaner. Yes, dry cleaners and marketing execs probably run in different circles, however the dry cleaner had a brother-in-law who worked for a restaurant chain that was getting ready to advertise for a marketing position. The networking between the marketing exec and the dry cleaner was plain and simple. When the dry cleaner asked the marketing exec how he was doing, the marketing exec mentioned that he was between jobs and he was looking for a restaurant marketing job. Ironically, the dry cleaner's brother-in-law worked for a restaurant chain and that's how the networking all started. The dry cleaner called his brother-in-law, confirmed the opening he had heard about when he was visiting his sister and brother-in-law, he confirmed the opening and then he put his dry cleaning customer (the restaurant marketing exec) in touch with his brother-in-law. The ball started rolling, and three weeks later, after three interviews, the marketing exec had a job he had been looking for.

In getting people into the networking mode, I always encourage them to develop a networking mindset. I tell them to "keep their eyes and their minds" open, to presume that anyone they meet can provide them with information that will help them to get their next job. And you should approach networking as a concept that is fun, even if you have an agenda. If you consider networking as burdensome, you're not going to do it. But if you go in with a positive attitude, you'll find that you enjoy connecting or reconnecting with people. Also, if you're unemployed or employed in a job that you don't like, you'll benefit from the support system offered by networking. Looking for a good job can often be depressing and you'll enjoy the encouragement and emotional support you can get from networking.

If you're going to be a good networker, you can't go through life with blinders on. You'll need to consider just about every person you meet as a candidate to help you in your job search.

Yes, there is an art to asking for help. Many of the daily interactions we have are very brief and you'll have to figure out a way to ask for help without coming across as pushy or overly aggressive. You'll have to figure out a style which fits your personality, but you can do that with practice.

In asking for job leads or information, you should remember that most people love to be helpful. It feels good to help others; you'll find that people will be glad to help you if they can. Anyone who has helped someone else realizes the satisfaction you can receive in doing that. Also, remember that people generally love to give advice and they like to be asked to give advice. It's natural that people like to be recognized for their expertise and for their potential to help others.

Whether you are unemployed, stuck in a crappy job or a low-paying job, you should remember that at one time or another, your network contacts have probably been in the same position. They'll be empathetic to your situation and, as a result, they'll be quick to help if they can.

And remember, networking is a two-way street. If you're going to ask for help, you should also be prepared to help the person you're asking for help. There's an old saying, "If you scratch my back, I'll scratch yours." That's a saying that describes the concept of networking.

Job Search

Networking is not just about helping yourself. It is also about helping others. As another saying goes, "Give and you shall receive."

After you've assembled your networking list, it's time for you to start "working" that list. If you're looking for networking assistance in finding a job, it makes sense that you should inform as many people as possible about your job search. Of course, if you already have a job and are looking for another, you're most likely going to have to have some discretion as you advertise the fact that you're looking for a new job. You might impair your chances of keeping your current job if you are openly advertising for another job. But if you're unemployed and find that there won't be any negative consequences in advertising that you are looking for a new job, I suggest that you start contacting as many people as possible as quickly as you can. Please remember that no one can help you find a new job if they don't know you are looking for one.

You should come up with a game plan on how you're going to ask for help from your network. If you're unemployed, you might consider informing your network of your search by posting a note on your social media platforms. You can do the same with your email contact list. And, with some people, you'll want to contact them personally by calling them, messaging them, or connecting with them in whatever means possible.

In requesting help in getting a job, the more specific you can be, the better off you'll be. Instead of the old "let me know if you hear of anything" line, you should be more specific in requesting help. If you are looking for an accounting job with a large accounting firm, you should mention that. If you are looking for a marketing position with a restaurant chain or a franchised chain, you should mention that.

And always keep your network updated on your progress in getting a job, especially those networkers who try to help you in your efforts. Let them know whether you got an interview or a job resulting from the information they offered. Always thank your networkers, regardless of the outcome and whether or not you got the interview or the job. I have a number of clients who update their networkers of their progress on a weekly basis through an email. One of those clients has even established a theme for her updates. She calls it "Finding a Job for Lisa" and sends out a humorous and light-hearted update to her network every week. In doing this, she continues to remind her networkers of her job search and she also gets them to invest in her efforts and success in finding a job.

I always caution people not to become "hit and run" networkers or "here today, gone tomorrow" networkers. It's important to continue to network even after you land a job. Again, networking is a two-way street and if someone is helpful, you shouldn't just take their help and run. The goal is to continue to network, as you never know when you'll need to use your network again. Also, you should offer to reciprocate any of the help you receive. If you can ever help someone in your network, you should do so. And, by all means, don't forget to thank those people who help you in any way.

One other thing I'd like to mention regarding the fundamentals of networking. You should prioritize your contacts and then decide on who you'll use as your references. In selecting possible job and personal references, you should obviously make sure that they will give you a reference that will allow you to secure the job you're hoping to get. I had a client who had difficulty in getting a job a few years ago. He went through a number of interviews, but could never land the job. In some of the interviews, he even got to the stage in which the prospective employer was calling his references. Finally, my client called one of the employers he had interviewed with and asked them why he didn't get the job offer that he had been expected. The employer hinted strongly that my client needed to double-check his references. My client later figured which one of his references had been providing "less than glowing" references and had, in fact, sabotaged my client's job search. To this day, my client still isn't sure whether these mediocre or negative references were intentional or not. But he quickly deleted this reference from his list as he proceeded with his job search.

Job Search

As you embark on your job search, you should make sure you ask your prospective references if they will vouch for you. With a phone call or a personal meeting, you can hopefully tell them what you are looking for and tell them what points you'd like them to highlight in acting as a reference for you. Also, you may want to keep them posted by sending them copies of your resume and cover letters, so you can make sure they are up-to-date with your job search efforts and also to get them to be more invested in your job search. Whether you send them a resume or not, it's important that you keep your references in the loop regarding your job search.

Ten Networking Questions to Ask. If you're new to networking or if you're not comfortable to do networking, I've listed some questions you might ask of the people you're networking with. When people ask me about the best ways to network, I always tell them that the most important thing to do in talking with another networker is to "be engaged". No, I'm not talking about a prospective marital situation, but I'm encouraging you to "be interested" in the conversation you're having. Give the person you're talking to your undivided attention. A number of years ago, I attended a networking event with a friend of mine and I was surprised to note that my longtime friend was doing a poor job of connecting to the people he was talking to. He wasn't making eye contact and he kept looking over the shoulder of the person he was talking to (maybe trying to identify the person he would talk to next). All in all, he seemed to be very disengaged and distracted. He definitely wasn't invested in the conversation he was having and I was sure the people he was talking to picked up on his lack of engagement.

After the networking event, I mentioned my observations to my friend, who I've always thought to have a short attention span. He was surprised that I had noticed this deficiency and he resolved to change his mode of operation. Months later when he and I talked, he told me that he had been to two subsequent networking events and he had made it a point to give the people he was talking to his undivided attention. He was pleased to tell me that he had already noticed that he was having more success as a networker. So, bottom line, when you're networking, make sure you are engaged with the people you're talking to.

Here are some questions you might use when you're networking with people who you don't already know:

1) **What do you do for a living?**
2) **Do you enjoy it?**
3) **How did you get into that? Did you have previous experience? Did you study that?**
4) **What company do you work for? How long have you worked for them? Is that a good place to work?**
5) **What's your favorite part of your job? What projects are you working on now?**
6) **What's next for you? Any career goals and objectives?**
7) **What do you like to do outside of work? Any interests or hobbies?**
8) **Do you do much networking?**
9) **Would you like to keep in touch?**
10) **How Can I Help?**

I love the "How Can I Help?" attitude. There's a popular television show on NBC called "New Amsterdam" in which the head of the New Amsterdam hospital has adopted the "How Can I Help?" mantra in his interactions with both staff and patients. Instead of just telling people what to do, he makes a point to always ask them how he can help. The people you're networking with are sure to appreciate your offer to help them with their careers and you'll likely make a great impression if you can adopt this attitude. However, please make sure you are sincere with your offer to help. And if you offer to do something for a fellow networker, you should make sure you follow through on your promises. Hollow promises or lip service without the follow through will be sure to tarnish your reputation as a networker.

In asking questions of fellow networkers, you'll find quickly that most people like to talk about themselves. And, in asking questions, don't have a firm set of questions to ask every one you speak with. Go with the flow of the conversation and let the direction of the conversation go wherever it takes you. A friend of mine was a member of a dating site and he recently had his first and only date with a woman who pulled out a written set of questions to ask him. Ultimately, he felt very uncomfortable with the situation and said that he felt like he was being interrogated. You won't want to do this when you are networking. Let the conversation take you where it takes you. Remember, networking is meant to be a casual activity, not an interrogation.

In asking questions of fellow networkers, you'll quickly find that asking questions will soon come naturally. And, chances are, if you become a proficient networker, you'll also become great at asking questions of prospective employers during interviews. Again, remember that people like to talk about themselves and if you can ask them the right questions, you will often find that people will think they had a great conversation, even if they did most of the talking.

How to Network If You're an Introvert. Studies show that about one-third of all people can be categorized as introverts. If you're an introvert, you may not look forward to networking. But, despite your concerns, introverts can still be proficient networkers. If you're an introvert, the most important thing for you to do in networking is for you to be yourself. Don't try to be someone you're not. You don't have to be the life of the party. You can get noticed and be an effective networker by being yourself.

I find that many introverts prefer smaller groups or one-on-one interactions. If you're an introvert, you might focus your attention to these smaller meetings or interactions, as you might well get lost within a larger group. And if you're at a networking event, remember that you're not the only person there who is scared or who is an introvert. You're not alone. With this in mind, you should note that there will be other introverts at the event who you can interact with. Introverts are often easy to identify. Kind of like wallflowers at a high school dance, you can probably identify introverts as those people who are off by themselves in a corner feeling awkward or buried in a large group and saying nothing. If necessary, you can gravitate toward other introverts, who will likely welcome your company. And remember, just because a person is an introvert doesn't mean that they don't have valuable contacts or have valuable information which can help you in your job search.

Another way for an introvert to be more successful at networking events is to find a "networking buddy", someone who can walk around with you as you meet other networkers. Introverts will often find it helpful to have a wingman or wingwoman. Even if you don't have a wingman, if you know someone else at the networking event, you should not hesitate to ask them to introduce you to other networkers. This should eliminate a lot of the initial awkwardness of being introduced to someone new.

And when you meet people, as mentioned earlier in this chapter, make sure you stay engaged in your conversation. Be there. Keep your phone in your pocket. Listen to what they say.

I know some introverts who even practice for networking events by coming up with a mental list of questions to ask the people they meet. This will help dispense with some of the stuttering and stammering which can often occur in meeting someone new.

I also encourage people, especially introverts, to set goals and objectives before any networking event. For example, one of my clients, always sets a goal to meet four new people and to connect with four other people he already knows at each networking event. If he can do this, he feels like he has been a successful networker for that event.

And, when you're at a networking event, make sure you don't wear out your welcome. After you've talked to someone for a while, be aware that you don't want to take up too much of their time, and move on to another networker. It's not prudent to dominate all of one person's time. After all, it is a networking event, and the goal is to meet a number of different people.

And, finally, in regards to introverts, I should mention that many introverts use the internet to network with other people. This includes people they don't yet know. You can meet new people online through professional network groups like those offered by LinkedIn. And, with people you already know, you can continue to network with them through email correspondence or social network presence and contact. As I say this, it should be pointed out that the most effective way to network remains face-to-face interaction, but online contact offers another means to network.

The bottom line is that just because you are an introvert doesn't mean that you can be a successful networker. There are ways to work around your inhibitions and the awkwardness of meeting other people. And, as you become more proficient at networking, you'll become more comfortable with it. Hopefully, it can become something that is fun for you instead of something you dread.

Whether you are an introvert or an extravert, you can benefit from the power of a strong professional network. When done well, networking can be a great tool for finding a new job…or jobs throughout your career. There's no doubt that people who are "connected" are often the most successful. When you invest in relationships, whether personal or professional, your investment will be likely to pay dividends throughout your life or your career.

Chapter 5—Shameless Self-Promotion

Self-promotion is the act of promoting or publicizing oneself or one's activities, in an orchestrated or intentional way. It's important for you to promote yourself and your talents, especially when it concerns your job search. I've heard it said before, "If you don't pat yourself on the back, no one else is going to do that for you." This thought is particularly appropriate for self-promotion. You could be one of the most talented people in your profession, however if no one knows that, it's unlikely that you will ever benefit from your talents and expertise. If you want to ensure career success, you'll likely have to spend some time promoting yourself and telling others about your strengths, talents, and abilities.

Identify Your Strengths. Before you promote your strengths, you're going to have to determine what they are. How do I do that, you ask. One of the best ways to do this is to simply take a look at your past job descriptions and use those as a starting point for listing the responsibilities of those jobs. In doing this, you should highlight responsibilities you've had in previous jobs, paying particular attention to the tasks you really enjoyed in those jobs. Also, take a look at the tasks which came naturally to you in those jobs, the tasks that were easy for you to learn. These are likely to be things that will help you identify your strengths.

For example, a client of mine is a public relations professional. She has worked for three different companies in which she's been responsible for promoting the company or organizing various company-sponsored events. This woman loves organizing events and taking them from start to finish. That's been a favorite part of the public relations jobs she's had, and her past experiences with that help identify event planning as one of her major strengths. On the less tangible side, this woman is a tireless worker who will do whatever it takes to complete a project to meet the assigned deadline. This also counts as one of her major strengths.

Another way for you to determine your strengths is to look back at previous job reviews and find out what superiors identified as your strengths. Also, your current and previous colleagues should be able to help you determine your strengths. If possible, I suggest that you ask these colleagues what they perceive to be your strengths and talents.

Another way to identify your strengths is to look at the areas in which your colleagues search advice or help from you. If they keep coming to you for your help or advice in any particular area, chances are that they view that area as one of your strengths. And, in determining strengths, it's also important for you to identify the tasks or projects which energize you. Do you find that you lose track of time on any of the tasks you have had in your current or past jobs? If so, this may well be something that you enjoy, something that is a strength of yours. At worst, it's something you definitely might want to pursue in future jobs. Ideally, in promoting your strengths as you look for another job, you should concentrate on the things you enjoy about your profession, not the things you dislike.

In identifying your strengths, it's important to note that skill and passion are not always connected. For example, I was an A Honor Roll student in high school, but I never had much interest in academics. Also, I was an all-conference baseball player even though I never had much of a passion for that sport. On the other hand, I had a real passion for basketball, however I was never as good at basketball as I was at baseball, as I was "vertically-challenged" at basketball, having to continually play against players who were much taller than I was. So even though something may be a strength of yours, if it's not also a passion, you may not want to self-promote that talent as you might pigeonhole yourself into jobs you're good at, but don't enjoy doing.

Personal Branding Tips That Bring Employers to You. The goal of personal branding in conjunction with any job search is to differentiate you from other people who may be applying for the same jobs. As I've mentioned before, having just a resume and a cover letter probably isn't going to be enough to get you the job of your dreams. With this in mind, many people are developing their own personal brand to enhance their image as an industry expert, to detail and complement their professional image, and to secure the jobs or projects they're looking for.

Personal branding is much like corporate branding. It gives you a chance to take an active role in managing and promoting your own image, instead of depending on what others say about you. In establishing your own personal brand, you'll be able to tell prospective employers and recruiters about your strengths, talents, and qualifications. You'll be able to convey who you are and who you want to be.

Before you start to establish your own brand, you will have to first determine what you want to be known for. For example, the Wendy's restaurant chain is well-known for its hamburgers. Although it advertises and sells other items such as chicken sandwiches, French fries, and soft drinks, the chain knows that hamburger sales are the key component to its success. The same goes for you in your personal branding. Although you may have multiple talents and abilities, you'll need to define your primary talents and abilities. You'll need to determine who you are and what you want to be. You'll need to determine what motivates you and what you can bring to the table for a prospective employer.

Then you'll need to determine who your audience is and how you're going to reach them. In a previous chapter, I've discussed at length the importance of a LinkedIn profile for most people who are looking to land a professional job. I've seen research numbers that indicate that over 90% of recruiters utilize social media platforms to find professional job candidates; almost all of these recruiters are using LinkedIn as the prime social media platform. The exception might be for extremely visual jobs for which a portfolio will do a better job of explaining what you do or what you've done. Photographers, artists, graphic designers, interior designers, and other like professionals are likely to benefit from some of the portfolio web sites we've previously detailed. However, even with the portfolio web sites, LinkedIn is a platform which allows people to link to portfolios or web sites. And some people will want to expand on their LinkedIn presence with their own personal web sites, blogs, podcasts, etc. Anything you can do to give prospective employers or recruiters a better idea of who you are and what your talents are will enhance your chances to get the job of your dreams.

As you go to establish your own personal brand, I suggest that you familiarize yourself with how the leaders or experts in your industry brand themselves. Check out their web sites, blogs, podcasts, magazine articles, and see how they are promoting themselves. In doing this, you'll pick up some ideas or methods that you'll want to imitate. You'll also want to develop your own twist for your personal brand and determine how you can improve upon the ways these other industry leaders are promoting themselves.

Another way to establish your brand is by requesting informational interviews with industry leaders. You'll be surprised at how accessible various industry leaders are. You'll find that many industry leaders are generous with their time and most of them will be genuine in providing you with information that will help your career. For those of you who are not familiar with the concept of an informational interview, it is an informal conversation in which one person will sit down with another person with the goal of obtaining career information from that person. An informational interview is not a job interview. In most instances, the party being interviewed will not even have a job opening.

I'll give you an example. I have a friend who had a restaurant marketing job in his early 20s. His goal was to parlay his marketing job into a sports marketing job. As a restaurant marketing associate, my friend would travel all over the country. Whenever he got the chance, he would research the major corporations in the city he was visiting to see if they had sports marketing departments. And then he would call to see if he could set up an informational interview with a sports marketing person. He wasn't looking for a job per se; he was primarily looking for information on how to get into sports marketing.

Job Search

He had tremendous success with his approach and he was able to get informational interviews with some marketing vice presidents and marketing directors from companies that either had sports marketing departments or people who were marketers for professional or college sports teams. My friend asked the people he met with about the paths they took to get their particular job and he asked for recommendations on how he might go about getting into the sports marketing profession. Those informational interviews were non-threatening to the person who gave the interviews; they offered the chance for one person to help another in getting into the profession of sports marketing. It should be pointed out that even though my friend met personally with many of these sports marketers, that was a time before video conferencing such as Skype or FaceTime was available. With today's technology, it's even easier to use video conferencing for an informational interview. And if video conferencing isn't an option, a simple telephone interview can also be effective, although not as effective as face-to-face or video.

Another tip for you to use in branding yourself is to develop what is known as an "elevator pitch". For those of you not familiar with an elevator pitch, it is simply a 30- to 60-second description of what you do. Imagine that you meet someone you haven't met before on an elevator, and they ask you what you do. You have only 30 seconds to a minute to convey to them what you do before the elevator stops and either you or the party you're speaking to has to get off the elevator. The same concept works well with networking, where you may have limited time to explain to someone what you do.

An online presence is almost a necessity for you to build your own brand. Besides LinkedIn, many people now have their own personal web sites or web pages. Those same people often use other social platforms such as Facebook or Twitter to promote themselves. With your online presence, it's extremely important that you consider what kind of image you want to convey with your personal branding. Also, it's important for you to remain consistent with the image you portray over the different platforms.

And there's more to personal branding than just online branding. As discussed previously, things such as networking and participation in various professional organizations or associations also offer opportunities for you to build your personal brand.

A friend of mine owns a promotional products company which sells imprinted promotion items such as t-shirts, caps, coffee mugs, pens, just about anything on which a corporate logo could be printed on. As part of his personal branding, he developed a cartoon character he named Promoman. Promoman is a cute and memorable character who wears a superhero's cape with a big P on his chest. My friend features that character on all of his company promotional materials. This form of branding has been very effective in getting customers and prospective customers to remember my friend's company. Another friend of mine owns a handyman business that performs various residential repairs, primarily for people who are not good at fixing things around the house. He calls himself Handy Dan and uses that moniker to brand himself and his one-man company.

Establishing a personal brand is not a "one and done" proposition. You will need to continue to review and update your personal branding, just as companies and corporations are continuously modifying or adjusting their brands. I'd recommend that you review your online presence at least once a month, even if you have a job. In doing this, you'll ensure that your brand remains fresh and doesn't become outdated.

Less-Known Strategies for Self-Marketing. Although I've already outlined the best-known self-marketing techniques, there are some additional ways in which you can build your personal brand. Below, I've listed some different ways you can promote your brand. Almost all of these techniques offer you inexpensive ways for you to enhance your brand.

--Seek recognition for your expertise. If you're knowledgeable in any particular area, you should establish yourself as an expert in that niche. The friend of mine who is a promotional products salesperson entered an association contest in which he won an award for a campaign he did for one of his clients. He received an award from the association for the creativity exhibited in that marketing campaign and he immediately leveraged that award by sending out a press release to the local newspaper and by posting that news on his social media sites and his personal web site. In doing so, he was establishing himself as an expert in the promotional products industry.

--Share your wisdom. If you have valuable information to impart, share it with others. The same promotional products salesperson mentioned above promotes his brand by conducting seminars at the national association trade shows. He has also appeared as a guest speaker at some of those shows, conferences, and conventions. Although he rarely gets paid for his efforts, he uses these opportunities to establish himself as an expert in his field.

I have two other acquaintances who enhance their brands by offering to conduct an hour-long radio show in which people can call in to the station to get advice. One of these acquaintances is in the computer repair business and, on a show called "Tech Talk", he takes calls from people who are having computer problems or are seeking computer advice. In return for his non-paid services, the station allows him to promote his own company/brand throughout the show. The other acquaintance is an automobile mechanic and he does something very similar, hosting a show called "Car Talk" in which he fields calls every Saturday morning from radio listeners who are experiencing car problems or have car questions. I've also heard similar radio shows from financial planners, gardeners, lawyers, stock traders, and real estate agents.

Besides radio shows, you can share your wisdom and promote your brand by writing your own blog, by writing guest blogs for other web sites, by posting comments on other blogs, by teaching a community education course. One of my clients has a passion for major league baseball and he runs a site which highlights his favorite major league baseball team. One of the things he does to build his brand is that he gets on various major league baseball blogs or forums and offers his opinion regarding some of those blogs or topics. In doing so, he often works in the name of his own site. However, he is not blatant in doing that, as he doesn't want his comment or content to get flagged as spam. The same guy writes guest blogs for other major league baseball web sites. He writes these guest blogs for free in return for being able to mention his web site at the bottom of his blog. And finally, he also appears as a guest "expert" on various local radio shows, where he talks about his local major league baseball team.

--Teach a class. Most communities or organizations sponsor classes in which people can become educated on various subjects. Again, most of these teaching gigs are non-paying gigs, however they'll allow you the opportunity to promote yourself as an expert in your field. My neighbor works for a bait and tackle store and he teaches a community adult education class on how to make your own fishing lures and flies. Another friend of mine teams up with a graphic designer friend to offer a community ed course on how to self-publish and market your own book. (The grapher designer instructs class attendees how to get an inexpensive cover design and how to format the book.) These two guys have also done this same course for some of the area libraries.

--Podcasts. My sister and her husband create podcasts on parenting and they've convinced a local radio station and a local tv station to provide links to their podcasts. A local appliance repairman has developed and posted some YouTube video clips in which he tells people how to repair various household appliances. Obviously, he deals mostly with simple repair problems, but he is well aware that people with more complicated problems will turn to him whenever they themselves can't fix something.

--Brand everything possible. Although no one would suggest that you have a tattoo of your brand on your forehead, you should be conscious of branding as many things as possible. If possible, place your name and personal letterhead on any correspondence you send out. The same goes for emails. If you are an accountant, instead of using a stock folder from the office supply store to hold a person's tax returns, you should make sure the folder is printed or contains a sticker with your own personal branding. If you are sending out a cover letter with your resume or a business proposal to prospective customers, or a thank you note to someone who granted you an interview, you should include your own personal brand whenever possible. The promotional products salesperson I've mentioned previously in this chapter even his a Promoman bobblehead character which he presents to customers who place orders of $1000 or more. This bobblehead character costs him less that $10 and offers him a way to keep his brand in front of his customer all year round.

--Keep in touch with your network. Birthday greetings, holiday greetings, thank you notes, and responding to posts on networking sites are all ways you can keep in front of your network. And don't limit you correspondence or self-marketing to professional contacts. Friends and family can also be a valuable part of your network.

--Be a community sponsor. Regardless of what community you live in or what online communities you participate in, most of those communities host events in which they are looking for sponsors or volunteers. These events offer you opportunities to promote your own brand. A friend of my wife has a side hustle gig in which she sells homemade salsa. She is trying to turn her side hustle into a full-time business. In an effort to build her brand, she often donates product to various organizations. For a local church festival, she donated salsa and chips for people to taste test at one of the festival booths. The people tasting her salsa could then register to win a year's supply of her salsa. In participating as a sponsor of the church festival, this woman was not only able to get lots of people to taste her product inexpensively, she was also able to build her brand inexpensively.

In summary, self-promotion is a mindset, an attitude. There are many different ways for you to build your own personal brand. Although you won't want to use all of the above self-promotion techniques, you should be able to use many of them in your attempts to establish yourself as an expert in your field and to create your own personal brand. And, best of all, with many of these techniques, you won't have to spend a lot of money to accomplish your goals. It's a simple matter of making yourself aware of the opportunities around you and then establishing a plan on how you're going to build your brand.

Chapter 6—Breaking Barriers

In providing you with tips and techniques on how to find a job, I realize that I might be a bit presumptuous in not pointing out that some of you might be fighting personal battles or inhibitions in searching for a job. Maybe you're sabotaging your own efforts to get a new job without even knowing it. Maybe you're someone who is prone to social anxiety or shyness and you find the thought of searching for a new job to be simply dreadful. Searching for a job, networking, creating an online portfolio, building a brand, and self-promoting…these are all activities that require the correct mindset and attitude. If you're not in the right mode of thinking regarding any of these tasks, you may be hindering your own chances of getting the job you want.

Four Ways You Might Be Sabotaging Your Own Job Search. Sometimes we inhibit our own efforts to getting a job, even without knowing that we are doing so. Here are a few common ways that people get in the way of their own efforts to get a job.

1) **You're using unrealistic language.** Some people make the mistake of using unrealistic language, especially in written correspondence such as cover letters. Over the years, I've had clients who have claimed to be "perfect fits" for the jobs they are applying for. Or they'll say in their cover letter, something like "I'm certain that you'll agree that I am highly qualified". With wording like this, you're not leaving any room for anything other than a yes or a no from the prospective employer. If I'm the person who is doing the hiring and I read a cover letter that says you are the "perfect fit" for the job I'm hiring for, my initial response is to say to myself, "Well, we'll see about that." Or if you're telling me you're certain I'll agree with something, you basically telling me that you're taking away my role as the person doing the hiring. Yes, it's okay to display an air of

confidence with your statements, but you're not likely to be successful if you are too brazen or cocky with the statements you make.

2) You're applying for jobs that you're really not qualified for. In determining which jobs you're going to apply for, it's important to set realistic goals. Yes, it's okay to dream big, but you'll have to be practical in determining your chances to get any given job, unless you want to waste your time or spin your wheels a lot during your job hunt. For example, if your current job is as an entry level marketing person, it's unlikely that you're going to be able to secure a vice president of marketing job for a major corporation. If you can be realistic in your expectations, you'll find that your job search will be much more efficient.

3) You're highlighting skills that are not related to the job you're applying for. If you have previous experience which centered around managing a large team of employees, but the job you're applying for does not include managing a team, then there's no reason to highlight that in your resume or your cover letter. It's okay to mention this experience if it is a major part of your work history, but don't place it near the top of your resume or highlight it in your cover letter. Or, if you speak Mandarin Chinese, but that has nothing to do with the job you're applying for, I wouldn't even mention it. In applying for any job, you should refer to the keywords in the job description or posting and then relate how your experience or expertise fits with what the prospective employer is looking for. Many job applicants make the mistake of not adapting their resumes to the jobs they are applying for. Be flexible with your resume. If one of the keywords in the job posting is management experience, and if you have management experience even if it wasn't your most recent job, you should not hesitate to move that management experience closer to the top of your resume…and also mention that experience in your cover letter. Be flexible in adapting your resume to the job you're applying for.

4) You're ignoring or trying to hide your lack of requirements. If you ignore your lack of qualifications for any particular job, you should know that such a deficiency may well hurt your chances to get that job. If you're lacking some of the experience or the qualifications that the prospective employer has noted in their job description, but you are still very interested in applying for that job, it will be best to approach that deficiency head-on. For example, if the job description highlights that the employer is looking for an individual who has had management experience and you don't have management experience, you should address this in your cover letter, instead of simply ignoring it or trying to hide that fact that you're lacking in this experience. You might say something like this in your cover letter: "Your job posting mentioned that you would like to hire someone who has management experience. Although I don't have any previous experience in managing a group of employees, I have always received performance reviews that compliment me as someone who can lead when necessary and someone who works well with others." In doing this, you'll be explaining your lack of management experience and, at the same time, acknowledging that this is experience they are looking for and then telling them that you don't expect that this will be an obstacle should you be hired for the job.

How to Overcome Social Anxiety and Shyness in Your Job Search. It's no secret that job hunting can be stressful. And it can even be more challenging if you are anxious or worried about the process. In my experience, there are two main things you should focus on in overcoming your anxiety.

First, it's important that you maintain a positive attitude throughout the process. If you're one of those people who tends to think negatively more than you think positively, you should make a constant effort to restrict your negative thoughts throughout your job hunting process. Try to turn your job hunting process into a positive experience instead of a negative experience. There's an old saying that is particularly applicable for this situation. "A problem is an opportunity waiting to happen." I suggest that you adopt that thought as your mantra throughout the job hunting process. If you can maintain a positive attitude throughout the process, you'll enjoy the process much more than you would if you let negative thoughts overwhelm you.

Second, in hunting for a job, you'll quickly find that whether or not you get a job is often beyond your control. You can't control whether a prospective employer offers you a job or not. With this in mind, it is important that you focus on the process of looking for a job instead of the outcome. I'm a big sports fan and I have heard numerous coaches tell their players to focus on the process, not the outcome. There are often huge discrepancies in the talents of many sports teams. A college football team that loses almost all of its games will have very little chance of beating a top ten team. So, coaches on the less talented team will often instruct their players to focus on the process, not the outcome. If a team works hard to try to become better, focusing on the process of doing that, they'll have a chance to get better and maybe someday they'll be able to compete with some of the much more talented teams. I recently heard a college football coach praising his team after they lost a game by the score of 56-7. "We worked hard all week and we limited our mistakes, but we just played a team that was bigger, stronger, and faster. If we can continue to work to get better week after week, I think we may be able to compete with them someday."

The same goes for job hunting. You may not be getting jobs because there are other applicants who have more experience than you. With a situation like that, it's important for you to stay positive and to focus on the process of getting a job, not the outcome. You can't change your history. If you're lacking in experience compared to other applicants, you can't change that. But if you can explain your lack of experience, someone is eventually going to give you a chance.

Here are some other tips and techniques to overcome anxiety you might have in searching for a job:

1) **Develop and implement a plan**. Maybe you're overwhelmed by how big of a project finding a job seems to be, especially at the outset of looking for a job. Most of us feel that way. The best way to minimize that problem is to come up with a step-by-step plan on how

you're going to "attack" the process of hunting for a job. If you can divide the overwhelming task of looking for a job into a set of smaller and more manageable tasks, the task of looking for a job will look a lot less daunting. You can take baby steps with this process, although you should assign a deadline to each of the projects so you can make sure you're moving forward and not procrastinating.

For example, maybe you just got laid off from your previous job. One of the first steps you'll want to take is to research the process of filing for unemployment. Subsequent tasks might include determining what kind of job(s) you want to apply for, creating a resume, developing or updating your online presence, researching job openings on some of the popular job sites, notifying your network of you impending job search, etc. If you can break down the complete task of looking for a job into individual projects like this, you'll find the process of looking for a job to be a lot easier and a lot less stressful. If you can do one or a couple tasks every day, you'll get closer to getting the job you want.

A friend of mine is a successful author who writes crime fiction books. He tells me the story that when he first decided he wanted to be an author, the thought of sitting down and writing a 500-page book was so overwhelming that he waited years to start writing his first book. He was able to do that only when he broke down all the tasks of writing a book into smaller, less daunting individual tasks, such as developing an outline, determining characters and the personalities of those characters, determining a setting and researching that setting, etc. After he did that, he resolved to write no less than 5000 words every day. (Other authors resolve to write one to three chapters every day.) His books average 90,000 to 100,000 words, so he knew that if he could produce 5000 words per day, he could complete a book in about 20 days. At the same time, he resolved write from 7 a.m. to 11 a.m. every day. (He prefers to write early in the morning so he then has time to spend with his family in the evenings. Other authors find that they are more productive in the evenings.)

You should take the same approach in your job search. I have many clients who resolve to spend a certain amount of time every day or

Job Search

every week looking for a job or preparing to look for a job. The time you spend looking for a job will obviously depend on whether you're currently employed or not. So, depending on how much time you have to look for a job, you should resolve to spend a certain amount of time every day or every week in looking for a job. Maybe it's five hours a day; maybe it's 20 hours a week. Some unemployed people even take the approach that looking for a job is their full-time job until they get one, so they'll work 40 to 60 hours a week at looking for a job. I have also had clients who resolve to apply for a specified number of jobs per week. Although most of these people understand that quality trumps quantity in any job search, they also understand that job hunting can be a bit of a numbers game and they know that the more jobs they apply for, the better chance they'll have of getting a job or at least an interview. A friend of mine who is a freelance writer has resolved to apply for a minimum of three writing projects every day. Sometimes, she gets multiple offers within a short period of time and she has to tell some prospective clients that she can't do their project immediately, but she finds it much easier to turn down a project than to have periods of time when she has no projects at all. In coming up with your plan to find a job, you'll have to figure out what works best for you, but I suggest that you come up with tangible goals and objectives to ensure that you're spending the right amount of time in looking for a job.

2)   Don't place all your eggs in one basket; don't count on a single opportunity. I am always surprised at how many people will wait until they have heard the outcome of one job application before they embark on another application. This is a major mistake, from a practical standpoint, an emotional standpoint, and a logistical standpoint. It doesn't make sense to let a situation control you when you can instead control the situation. Even if you've applied for your dream job, you have to remember that you're not the one who gets to decide whether you get the job or not. That lies with the prospective employer. With that in mind, you should make sure that you continue to move forward in your job search, applying for multiple jobs if possible. If you are fortunate enough to get multiple job offers from your applications, you'll be in an enviable position, able to choose the job you prefer. Remember that prospective employers are interviewing multiple candidates; there's no reason for you not to be exploring multiple opportunities at the same time.

3)   Look for jobs when you have jobs. The best time for you to look for a job is when you have another job. It's a lot less stressful and you'll find that you're in a much better position in deciding whether or not to take a new job. This being said, I am always surprised at how people do not like to do this. As an example, a company in a neighboring community announced that it was closing one of its factories two years in advance of the closing. They did this with the idea that their employees would then have plenty of time to look for other employment. The company even offered classes and an allowance for employees to be trained in other professions. Yet, when the plant finally closed, only 37% of those employees had taken advantage of this extremely generous offer from the employer. In fairness, some of the employees who didn't take advantage of the offer were near retirement age and they opted to take an early retirement. However, a majority of the employees there were going to wait until there current job expired before they embarked on a new job search. Unfortunately, this happens all too often with most people. You need to remember that it's much, much easier for you to look for a job if you already have another job. You have a lot more leverage and it's a lot less stressful. Even if you can allocate only a couple hours a week to searching for your next job, networking, updating your social media, or creating your brand, you'll be better off if you can do so while you're employed.

4)   Practice interviewing. Before any interview, I strongly suggest that you prepare yourself. Research the company you're interviewing with; try to determine what interview questions you might be asked and determine what your answers will be to those questions. When I've interviewed for jobs, I've always conducted an internal dialog in which I imagine what questions might be asked of me and my responses to those questions. Other people will use friends, family, or colleagues for that process. Another way to get ahead of the interview game will be to research common interview questions on the internet. Anything you can do to practice for your interview should enhance your chances for success.

5) **Don't dwell on negative thoughts and scenarios.** Again, a positive mindset is extremely important in the job search process. It's important for you not to let negative thoughts overcome your positive thoughts. In applying for jobs, you're dealing with outcomes that you can't control, so the goal should always be to focus on the process, do the best you can, and let the chips fall where they may. I have a friend of mine who is a pessimist by nature. He often imagines worst case scenarios instead of best case scenarios. He told me the story of an interview he had for his first job after he graduated from college. He was applying for a public relations job. For whatever reason, the prospective employer had all four of the people who were to be interviewed show up at around the same time. So, all four candidates were sitting together in the lobby. My pessimistic friend quickly determined that he was the only recent college grad among the four candidates. He also noticed that while he was wearing his off-the-rack interview suit, the other candidates seemed to have better clothes to wear for the interview, and instead of vinyl portfolios, they were carrying leather briefcases. Upon seeing this, my friend presumed that his die was cast; he'd have very little chance of competing with these other candidates. Ends up, he got the job. The woman who did the hiring later told him that she was open to someone who hadn't already established bad habits in another job; she liked the fact that he wasn't as polished as the other candidates, but had expressed a sincere interest in learning the ins and outs of the job and working hard. She also thought that his personality would be a better fit with the other people on the public relations team. The moral of the story: Don't let your negative thoughts control you, especially in a process you can't control. You never know why a prospective employer will hire one person over another. So, it's a waste of time to dwell on the reasons why someone won't hire you.

6) **Consider hiring the services of a career coach or counselor.** If you have the budget to do so, many people benefit from the use of a career coach.

7) **Have an explanation for your social anxiety.** One of my clients suffers from extreme social anxiety. This affects him when he is speaking in front of large groups and it affects him during the one-on-one interview process. He and I talked extensively about how to solve this problem. He acknowledges that his anxiety is mostly related to a fear of failure. His social anxiety is so bad that he sweats profusely when he is placed in some social situations. Although I have never accompanied him to an interview, he has told me that, on occasion, he has experienced flop sweat similar to the sweat that actor Albert Brooks experienced as a television news broadcaster in the movie "Broadcast News". In the movie, Brooks' character was sweating like a running faucet as he did his first newscast. My friend tells me that he has had to have a handkerchief in hand before during interviews because he was sweating so much. He's also had shirts that have been soaking wet. So, for him, the way his anxiety manifests itself so severely that he's lost numerous job opportunities as a result. However, now whenever he goes on interviews, he is quick to explain his problem. He is quick to point out that he experiences anxiety in interview situations and tells them that "Some people don't think that I interview well because of the anxiety I have during the process. If you can get past my anxiety, you'll find that I will be a loyal, hardworking, and conscientious employee who will sincerely value the job opportunity you're offering." With this explanation, you'll note that he is facing his anxiety head-on instead of trying to hide it. His last two employers have been able to get past his anxiety and have hired him despite this misgiving. I've had other clients who have also broached their social anxiety or shyness with prospective employees by saying, "I am a shy person, and I sometimes don't come across well in interview situations, however I can assure you that I will be a valued

employee here. I may not have much style, but I can assure you that I have plenty of substance."

8) Utilize a support system. The job search process is often a difficult process and you'll certainly be able to take some of the anxiety out of that process by finding someone to talk to or to support you during this process. Many people who are looking for a job decide to make the process a solitary process and then they find that the process is depressing because they have no one to discuss their feelings with. Don't hesitate to ask family, friends, or colleagues to lend moral support during your job search. And, don't forget that almost all of us have gone through the job search process and it's not difficult to find someone who is familiar with the trials and tribulations of finding a job.

Develop an Attitude that Attracts Success Now. Success is all about attitude and effort. You should know that success doesn't happen to you…it happens because of you. Success is something you have to earn. Most people don't automatically attract success. People attract success because they work hard to achieve it. They make sacrifices and they consistently strive to become a version of their better self.

I've previously mentioned the mindset in which a person views problems as opportunities. This is extremely important for people who want to become more successful. People with the "problem is opportunity" mindset will find it much easier to inspire faith, confidence and trust in others.

People who are successful have the ability to "attack" problems instead of letting those problems control them. I'll give you an example. One of my clients was about to embark upon a job hunt. She asked me for my recommendations about how she should go about establishing an online presence that would enhance her chances of getting a great job. This woman was smart, but she wasn't technically-oriented. I was very surprised to find out that she has set up her own personal web site, created some podcasts, and created some blogs within just a short period of time. I asked her what her mindset was in creating her online presence and she said, "I viewed it as an opportunity to teach myself some new skills. I attacked these projects with a 'can do' attitude. I knew going in that there was information available on the internet on how to do each of those tasks, so I simply did my research and I learned how to do it." This is a woman who will attract success, because she is willing to do the necessary work to achieve it.

Another way to achieve success is to fail. Yes, you can achieve success by failing. There's an old saying, "When you fail, you learn. When you fail more than anyone else, you learn more than anyone else." Success is the direct result of the number of experiments you perform. If you're trying things and failing, you're likely to eventually be successful. On the other hand, a person who never tries is unlikely to ever succeed.

A few other tips on how you can start to attract success:

    --Be authentic, genuine, and vulnerable. Don't be afraid to admit when you don't know something; don't be afraid to learn new things.

    --Be a giver instead of a taker. Most people are takers. They'll take anything they can get, even if they don't need it. But you'll find that giving time and effort without expecting anything in return can be a key factor in positioning you for professional success.

    --Shut up and listen. Always remember that you can learn a lot more by listening than you can learn by talking. So many people are intent upon showing other people how much they know that they often forget to listen what other people have to say.

Again, attracting success is all about attitude and effort. If you have the right mindset, if you're willing to give instead of receive, if you're willing to listen, if you're willing to learn and not afraid to fail, then you'll be a lot more likely to attract success.

Chapter 7—Job Interview Secrets

I doubt that I'll surprise anyone when I state that the interview is a critical part of the interview process. If you've ever lost a job opportunity because you didn't interview well, you'll be well aware of what a disappointment it is to get that far along in the job search process and then not get the job because you didn't make the impression you wanted to make. In this chapter, I'm going to give you some advice on how you can make the best possible impression in your interviews with prospective employers.

Golden Rules to Make an Excellent First Impression in a Job Interview. There are a lot of different things you can do to ensure that you have the best possible chance to get a job based on your interview.

‑‑**Make sure you're prepared.** First of all, do your research. Research the company you are interviewing with by visiting their web site and by doing an internet search to find additional information on the company. Research the person you are interviewing with, checking for a LinkedIn profile, social media, and an internet search. Determine what kind of dress attire the company has and then select appropriate attire. If you're interviewing with a law firm, you're likely to dress different than you would if you were interviewing with an internet startup company. If you're not sure what would be appropriate attire, call the receptionist at the company you'll be interviewing with, tell them you have an upcoming interview, and ask them what the normal dress attire is there.

Make sure you know exactly how to get to the location where the interview will be conducted and then calculate the amount of time it's going to take to get there. (I've taken test drives before to determine how long it will take to reach an interview location. Don't forget to account for heavier traffic at different times of the day; likewise, don't forget to account for road construction on your route.) Being late for an interview will probably be a deal-breaker. Many years ago, when I was hiring for a small company I owned, I passed on a candidate simply because she was 10 minutes late. She apologized immediately when she arrived, telling me that her husband, who had delivered her to the interview, was running late. Immediately, I thought to myself that if the job wasn't important enough for her husband to get her to the interview in time, then that could present a problem in the future. Turns out that she was the best candidate and I liked her slightly better than the other candidates, however I ruled her out because she was late for her interview.

And, although you're probably already familiar with the job posting or the job description, make sure you review multiple times and remember the keywords from the posting. Highlight those keywords in your interview and make sure you explain any areas of expertise you have in those keyword areas.

--When you meet the person who will be interviewing you, make sure you greet them with a firm handshake (not a floppy fish handshake) and also make sure that you make solid eye contact with that person. This may not seem important to you, but this first 30 seconds of the interview process is very important to some interviewers. I'll confess that I will give bonus points to people I meet who have a firm handshake, eye contact, and a bright smile.

--Be observant. It's important that you are able to be aware of your surroundings and also the person you are interviewing with. If you're waiting for your interview in the lobby of a company, observe what's going on. You can tell a lot about the culture of a company just be seeing how employees interact with each other in the lobby. Also, how does the receptionist handle phone calls? If he or she treats each caller as if they are an interruption, that might be a sign that there's something wrong with the company culture. I once had a job interview for which I waited in the lobby for almost a half-hour, as I was early for my interview and the interviewer was conducting another interview. In the 30 minutes I spent in the lobby of this company, I determined that the company I was hoping to work for was probably not a good place to work. The receptionist wasn't all that friendly and almost all of the employees who came through the lobby had negative demeanors. So, use your time in the lobby to check out the corporate culture.

Along the same lines, you need to be able to read the person you're interviewing with as the interview transpires. Is the interviewer a serious person? Is their style formal or casual? Do they have a sense of humor? Are they truly interested in your answers to the questions they're asking or are they just moving down a checklist? Is the conversation flowing smoothly or is it a bit uncomfortable? Either way, you'll have to analyze what's happening as it happens, and then you may have to make adjustments accordingly to increase the comfort level of the interview or to find common ground. In finding common ground, I encourage you to look around the office of the interviewer if you get the chance. Most people have some personal effects displayed in their office. You might see things like family photos, bowling or golf trophies, framed diplomas or degrees, etc. If you can find common ground with any of these personal effects, use that information appropriately during the interview. For example, if you see a photo of the interviewer with her daughter and you have a daughter also, that might be something you can talk about, if there is an opening to do so. If you see a golf trophy and you're a golfer, you should see if you can find common ground with that. Although it's very unlikely that you'll get a good job because you are an avid golfer, if you can convey that common ground to your interviewer, he'll be more likely to remember you. Don't underrate "common ground" in connecting with a prospective employer.

--Don't babble; don't be curt; don't be afraid to tell brief stories as to why you're the right fit for the job. If the interviewer is interrupting you during your answers, that's probably a sign that you're babbling or your answers are too long. On the other hand, if the interviewer is pausing without talking after your answer, he or she is probably waiting for you to expand on your answer. And, remembering that an interview is meant for you to expand on your resume and cover letter, it's often advisable to tell a story or two as to why you are the best candidate for the job. However, with any stories you tell, make sure that you're not longwinded in doing so. If the interviewer wants you to tell them more, they'll let you know by asking additional questions related to your story.

--Be positive. Be enthusiastic. One of the most common mistakes people make in interviews is that they will spend a lot of time ripping their current job or employee. In doing this, the interviewer may well think that this is how you'll be talking about her or her company when you interview for your next job. It's OK to say what you don't like about your current job or the current company you work for, especially if you are asked about it, but I would strongly suggest that you show some decorum in doing so and that you don't dwell on these negatives throughout the interview. Always try to be enthusiastic and positive when discussing the job you are applying for.

--Assorted common sense tips. If you have previous work to show, bring samples of that work. For example, if you are a photographer or a graphic designer, you'll want to bring a portfolio of your work to the interview. If you're an advertising professional, you may want to bring photos or samples from an ad campaign you worked on. And, pay attention to the vessel or container you use to hold these samples or portfolio. I've had an interviewee bring in his portfolio in a grocery bag; I've had a lady dump out most of the contents of her huge handbag on the conference table as she looked for a photo to show me. (It looked like she was getting ready to host a garage sale.) Make sure you turn your phone off and put it away during the interview. And, if you're going to wear perfume or cologne, go light on it. Please remember that just about every office has someone who detests fragrances, even pleasant fragrances. Make sure you have the correct name of the person who is interviewing you and make a point to use that name at least occasionally throughout the interview. If you are interviewing with multiple people, get all the names, writing them down, if necessary. Using someone's name is one of the most basic ways you can use to establish a connection. And make sure, you use peoples' names when you depart the interview. That leaves a good impression. i.e.—"Josh, thanks for your time today. Mike and Joe, I enjoyed meeting you."

--Close out your interview; find out what the next step is. Don't leave an interview without thanking the interviewer for their time. And don't leave an interview without finding out what the next step is. When will they be making their decision? Will they call you or how will they inform you about the outcome of the interview? Is it OK for you to call them to follow up? If so, when can you call them?

--Follow up. Follow up immediately with a "thank you for the opportunity to interview note". I recommend a snail mail note that is handwritten if it's a short note or typed if it's a longer note. I discourage emails, as they can be too easily deleted. I prefer paper notes or thank you cards, because the recipient is likely to hang on to them for a while before disposing of them. And then in following up with phone calls, make sure you contact the interviewer when he or she told you to call them. And try to remain visible without becoming a nuisance.

Expert Tips to Stand Out in a Competitive Market. If you've reached the interview phase of a job search, you've already placed yourself above other candidates who did not get interviews. But now the going may get tougher as you compete against candidates who have been deemed to be more qualified than the others who have been left behind. There are still some things you can do to leverage your position as you head into your interview.

--Do your research. Just last week I had a human resources professional tell me how she views a person who has done his research going into an interview. "It's refreshing to meet with a candidate who knows what they're talking about and who has already researched the company. It's nice not to have to spend all of my interview time describing my company to the person I'm interviewing." The same human resources person told me that she also checks to see if the applicant has customized his resume and cover letter for the job he is applying for. "If they haven't taken the time to do that and they are using a generic resume and cover letter, I tend to think that they may not be all that interested in the job opportunity we have to offer."

--Provide links to your online brand. If you've cleaned up your online media presence (i.e.—your social networks), then it might be a good idea to provide links to your personal web site or portfolio, you're LinkedIn profile, your Facebook and Twitter pages (if appropriate), your blogs, your podcasts, or any articles on the internet which show you in a positive light. The person doing the hiring is likely to do this anyway, but in providing links to your information, you'll make their job easier and, more importantly, you'll be able to "control the narrative"/control the information the interviewer sees. I've had clients who provide this information a few days in advance of the interview through an email and that seems to work well for them. If the interviewer is going to do his or her homework before they interview you, you'll have made their job easier and you'll be able to control the narrative.

--Personality and attitude. In the interview itself, make sure you find a way to show your personality. It may surprise you, but many employers admit to hiring personality and attitude over experience. They're looking for someone who is going to be passionate and enthusiastic about working at their company. So, when you go into your interview, make sure you go in with a positive attitude and make sure you show your enthusiasm toward the job you're applying for. As another hiring manager once told me, "It's hard to fake an eager attitude. We always look to see how eager an applicant is about the job we're offering."

--Accomplishments and results over skills. Always concentrate on your accomplishments and results over your skills. Your skills are already listed on your resume. If you have specifics to show your accomplishments in previous job, be specific. The same goes for any results you've produced in previous jobs. Some examples: A brand manager instituted a brand campaign which increased the sales of a product by 11%; a football coach took a program that won two games the season he was hired to a program that won nine games only three years later; a management team professional took a department that had a 65% turnover rate to a department that had only 12% turnover in his tenure; a salesperson for a product line increased sales of that product by 32% within a year. The same goes for any accomplishments you may have achieved: Employee of the year in a company of 120 employees; won an industry award for a public relations campaign; president of a college chapter of professional journalists; editor of the college newspaper. You get the picture. In listing specific accomplishments, awards, and achievements, you'll be able to offer some tangible proof on why you're the right person for the job. This will allow the interviewer to put some specifics behind the skills you list on your resume.

The 10 Job Interview Questions You Should Always Know How to Answer. Whether you get the job you're looking for may well depend on how you handle or answer the questions that are asked of you. Although you can never be sure what questions you'll be asked, there are some standard questions that you should definitely be able to answer. And if you know you to answer these basic questions, you'll be much better prepared to answer any questions you might get. As a matter of fact, I would suggest that you use these basic questions in preparing for every job interview you have.

When I was fresh out of college, I lost a job opportunity because of the way I answered what should have been a simple question. The interview was going well until near the end of the interview when the hiring manager asked me "How my family members would describe me?" It was a simple question, but I totally blew it when I used the "L" word. I told the interviewer that "My sister might say that I'm lazy". Yes, I referred to myself as lazy in an interview. I don't know why I said it and there was no truth to it, but I said it. When I said it, I knew immediately that I could stick a fork in my chances of getting the job I wanted. I tried to walk back my statement, but the die had already been cast. Although I don't expect you to botch a question like I did, I'm going to be quick to tell you that it is important for you to run through how you will answer questions in an interview before you have the interview.

Below I've listed some basic interview questions which you're likely to run into over the course of your interviewing career. Although I personally consider some of these questions to be mundane, the basic premise of these questions is for the interviewer to get to know you and to find out if you're a good fit for the job they are offering. The goal is simply to get you to talk and then the answers you give will possibly separate you from the other applicants, either positively or negatively.

1) **Can you tell me about yourself?** This is a very common question and I suggest that you definitely have a practiced elevator pitch in answering this question. In the period of a minute or two, you should be able to tell them who you are, emphasizing who you are professionally over who you are personally. And you should do so with confidence.

2) **Why do you want to work here?** This question provides you with a chance to show that you've done your research on the company you're interviewing with and the job you're interviewing for.

3) **How did you find out about this job?** If you have a personal connection, this is a good spot to use it.

4) **Why are you looking for another job when you already have one?** In answering this question, emphasize the positive aspects of the job you're interviewing for, not the negative aspects of your current job.

5) **Why should we hire you?** Here's your chance to tell what you can bring to the table and what places you above other applicants. Be specific whenever possible.

6) **Where do you see yourself in five years?** I'll admit that I detest this question, but it is one of the most frequently asked interview questions. If you have a specific plan, outline it briefly to the interviewer. If you don't know where you're going to be in five years, it's OK to say that you're not exactly sure what's going to happen, however you feel that this job will be a definite help in advancing your career path.

7) **Tell me about a conflict or disagreement you've had at work and how you handled that conflict?** This question is designed to determine how you can think on your feet and how you react to conflict. You should definitely have a prepared answer to this question, and always use an example in which you were able to resolve the problem with a satisfactory solution or compromise.

8) **What's your dream job?** Be honest in your assessment of what your dream job is, but hopefully include how the job you're applying for will help you get that dream job.

9) **What are your salary requirements?** Some employers ask this question; others don't. Either way, you should definitely know what your salary expectations are for any job you apply for.

10) **Do you have any questions?** Almost all interviews feature this question near the end of the interview. You should always have at least a couple of questions to ask in response to this question. Instead of saying that you don't have any questions or that the information the interviewer has provided has answered all of your questions, this "do you have any questions" question offers you the chance to show that you've been engaged in the interview process and a chance to stand out among other job candidates. Hopefully, you can develop questions as the interview has progressed. If not, you should go in with three to five questions to choose from and then select a

question or two from that list. In asking questions, you should know that many interviewers enjoy this part of the interview, as it allows them a chance to deviate from the formal part of the interview and to talk about their company or themselves. So, the more relevant your questions are, the better chance you'll have to place yourself above other applicants.

Chapter 8—Make It Happen

Whether you are changing careers, negotiating a salary, or following up on your job application, here are some things to think about when you are doing so.

What You Need to Know if You're Changing Careers. Are you at that point in your career when you are ready to make a career change? If so, there are definitely some things you need to consider before making such a move.

Most importantly, I suggest that you plan for any career move. Some people make the mistake of jumping impulsively into a new career, possibly because they don't like their current career. That's a mistake that can increase the likelihood of failure in your new career. You should research thoroughly any new career or vocation you are about to embark upon. Find out what kind of education or training is required or recommended for this vocation. Research what kind of earnings you might expect from such a career. Review your current financial situation to make sure you have enough resources to subsidize a new career. Research the new career you desire by using the internet and by hopefully connecting with people who are already in that career. Informational interviews (discussed earlier) are in invaluable resource for learning about any new career you are interested in.

If you have a spouse or significant other, are they on the same page with this possible career change? Certainly, any career change warrants multiple discussions with those people who are important to you.

In embarking on a new career, you should know that you may have to take a hit financially to get into a new career. If you are at a management level in your current career, you may have to start at an entry level or a lower level in a new career and this is likely to affect your income level. Do you have ways in which you can finance a new career? Maybe you will need to dip into your pension plan, your retirement savings plan, or your savings account. Maybe you will need to take out a second mortgage on your home. Or maybe you will need to take a part-time job to subsidize your new career, at least in the initial stages of the new career. Will you need to make any lifestyle changes to accommodate a new career? Longer hours? Less family time? More travel? If so, are these sacrifices you'll be willing to make? You should know that financial factors are the major reason people do not embark upon new careers. Financial strain, lack of financial planning, and debt can easily quash any career dreams or aspirations you might have.

Although you might be anxious to jump full throttle into a new career, I suggest that you consider whether you can get into that career in stages. For example, I have a close friend who was a corporate marketing executive for years. He'd spent a lot of time in a highly volatile industry where he was paid well but he found that he was a victim of layoffs frequently during these marketing stints. He was always a good and valued employee, but he was in a career in which there is a lot of turnover. Finally, he decided that he wanted a career in which he could control his own destiny. He also wanted the chance to get out from behind his desk in a job that was more tangible. His dream was to start a tree trimming and removal company. Yes, that's a major change from being a corporate marketing executive. Although he had helped trim and remove trees when he was younger, he really didn't know the ins and outs of that industry. He contacted various people who owned tree trimming companies, told them of his aspirations, and picked their brains on how he might go about getting into the industry. He was amazed at how helpful and forthcoming these other business owners were in telling him all about the plusses and minuses of the industry. As there aren't many classes teaching people how to trim and remove trees, he found an owner who allowed him to work as a paid apprentice on weekends while he continued with his marketing job. He did this for three months until he had enough knowledge to start his own company. He got his wife on board with his career move and she eventually became his scheduling coordinator and marketing person. Years later, he has a very successful career, with three different crews of employees who work for him in trimming and removing trees.

I did the same thing with a company I started many years ago. Instead of quitting my current job immediately, I hired a friend of mine who was between jobs and, based on my direction, she found an office location for me, priced out and purchased my office supplies and furniture, coordinated the development of my advertising and marketing materials, pre-interviewed secretarial candidates, etc.

In changing careers, you should also have a support system or a mentor that can either help you with your move or can be there as a sounding board. I strongly suggest that you enlist other people to help you as you make this career transition. It can be extremely difficult to embark on a new career, especially if you've been in another career for a while. If you can get your network or a mentor engaged in your transition, you'll have a much easier transition, especially emotionally.

Also, in changing careers, be prepared for setbacks. Always remember that things seldom go as planned. I've started two different companies that have experienced setbacks on two different sides of the spectrum. With one company, I'd had friends who had indicated that they would become clients of mine when I started my own company. But after I did start my company, I found that they were very slow to throw any business my way and that created a major financial strain to the point where I had to rent out my home and move into an apartment for a brief period of time. Finally, the people who had promised me business came around and my business flourished. I realized later that they were reluctant to give me business immediately after I started my company, as they wanted to wait and see if I was going to stay in business. On the other end of the spectrum, I started another business in which I had thought I had enough funds to finance the company for a period of six months, until I established the business. Three weeks into the start of my business, I received a huge order that I hadn't expected and I needed to use all of the funds I had saved for the venture to purchase products required to fill the order. And I needed more funds than I even had. Although it was a nice problem to have, it was a polarizing problem as I hadn't established a line of credit with a bank to finance the order. Thankfully, I was able to think outside the box and I got my customer to pay me in advance for the huge order in return for a discount on the merchandise. It should be pointed out that most companies would not have prepaid an order before the merchandise was delivered, as that wasn't a common industry practice. Bottom line was that I got very lucky with this order. So, in planning for a new career, you need to account for both worst case scenarios and best case scenarios.

And one more thought on changing careers: If you want to make a career change, but you're not sure what new career you want for yourself, you should be sure to evaluate the skills and the passions you've had in your past career. Take a look at the things you've done well or liked in your past career (also the things you have disliked) and use that information in determining a possible new career. Ideally, you'll be able to parlay some of your skills and passions into a new career. If you make a 180-degree change in careers and are not able to utilize some of your previous experience in your new career, your transition is going to be much more difficult.

Seven Negotiation Techniques to Get the Salary You Desire. After you've successfully moved past the initial interview stage and your prospective employer is ready to extend an offer, it's time to talk salary. Although some people liken the salary negotiation process to the negative experience of buying a car, you'll can't bypass this process in finalizing your job search. You'll want to make sure that you are getting a fair price for your services, regardless of what job you take. Here are some simple tips and techniques for you to use in determining what salary you deserve and then negotiating for that salary.

1) **What is your market value?** It's important that you research what other people in your field are paid, both on a national and local level. You can consult salary guides on the internet. Or if you have a relationship with a recruiter, you might ask them what the salary ranges are for your career field. And always remember that where

you're located will probably impact your salary, especially in regards to cost of living. A job in San Francisco or New York City is likely to pay more than the same job in a small town in Iowa, just because of the cost of living. Also, know what the market is for your particular job. If your prospective employer is having difficulty hiring for the position your interested in, you have a lot more leverage than you do if it is easy for them to hire for that position. You should keep this in mind going into any salary negotiation.

2)   **Don't say yes or no too early or too late.** Make sure you discuss salary before you take the job. If you take the job before you've reached a salary agreement, you've lost any leverage you might have in that regard. And if you delay in accepting an offer, the hiring manager might get frustrated and move to another candidate.

3)   **It's not all about you.** Please remember that, in regards to your salary negotiation, your personal needs are going to have very little impact on the salary you are offered. A friend of mine who is a hiring manager recently had a prospective employee tell him that he required a specific salary so he could make his house payments and car payments. That's an absolute no-no. Your personal needs are not the concern of the hiring manager.

4)   **Give a specific salary.** If a prospective employer asks you what salary you will expect or require in your new job, give them a specific salary or, at worst, a tight salary range. Don't tell someone that you want an annual salary of $60,000 to $90,000, as that's a very large range. If you offer a range, make it tighter. i.e.--$70,000 to $75,000. And remember that if you're giving a range, you're likely to get the salary on the lower end of the range you're requesting. And, one other thing, when an employer asks what salary you are expecting, act confidently without being pushy. For example, you might respond as follows: "I've researched what other people in similar positions earn and, based on that, I was hoping for something in the $70,000 to $75,000 range. Is that possible?"

5)   Don't overlook the benefits. Negotiating a compensation package often involves more than just salary. You should concern yourself with other compensation benefits and perks, which might include moving expenses, health insurance, vacation allocation, retirement savings plans, professional development opportunities, and advanced education benefits. With some of these benefits, the company you're interviewing with will have an established policy that they won't be willing to deviate from. i.e.—A company is not going to change its health insurance benefits because you don't like their current benefits. But, nevertheless, it's important for you to know what those health insurance benefits are. On the other hand, some companies do have flexibility with some compensation benefits, such as moving expenses, signing bonuses, and vacation time. If an employer doesn't have the flexibility to meet your salary requirements, maybe they have flexibilities in these other areas. If you are fortunate enough to have multiple job offers, you should obviously include benefits in your comparing these offers.

6)   Honesty is the best policy. Don't inflate salaries from previous jobs. Don't make up competing job offers. If a prospective employer finds out that you've been dishonest, you're likely to become "history" with that employer.

7)   Get your offers in writing. Once you and your future employer have agreed to a salary and a compensation package, make sure you request a written detail of that offer. That document should obviously be addressed to you and it should be signed by your employer. Unfortunately, I've heard of some instances in which an employer and an employee have a misunderstanding regarding salary and benefits and then the employee is often left at a disadvantage because he or she doesn't have written documentation of what was originally promised.

How to Follow Up on a Job Application the Right Way. If there is a job you're really interested in, you're probably going to be anxious to find out what's going on with the application you submitted. As a job applicant, you'll have to remember that, unlike the company doing the hiring, you're not in control of the process. This may be frustrating at times, but you should always remember that there are some right ways to follow up on your applications.

People often ask about what is the appropriate time frame to follow up after you've submitted your application. Normal time to follow up is about a week later. You can follow up in a number of ways, including phone, emails, or a LinkedIn message. If you are calling the company you're interested in working for, make sure you are prepared for what you're going to say, whether you speak to the hiring manager or whether you are leaving a voice message. Many people practice what they're going to say or will even have a few written notes on hand when they make the follow up phone call.

In following up, always be polite and professional. If you leave a bad impression, you'll likely be out of the running for the job before you even get an interview. Always make your messages brief, especially with phone calls. Appreciate the fact that peoples' time is valuable and they probably won't be interested in a long, rambling diatribe. That being said, there's no harm in including a sentence or two telling them why you are a good fit for their job offering. Anything that can place you above other candidates might well help you gain an interview. And, of course, with any correspondence you send, whether via voice mail or email, make sure to leave your name and phone number or email address.

Although it's OK to follow up multiple times, you should make sure you don't become a nuisance. And if you've tried multiple times to get a response without success, you may eventually have to concede to the idea that they're not interested in you.

Conclusion

If you've read this book, you now have the tools you'll need to get the job of your choosing. If you can follow the tips that apply to your job search, you'll be successful in your search…if not immediately, then eventually. In reading self-help books like this one, there are two types of people: those who will take the valuable information offered and implement it; those who will place this information on the back burner, saying they'll implement it when they get around to it…but then they never get around to it. I implore you not to be one of those people who never gets around to it.

You now know how important it is to "attack" what looks like the overwhelming task of finding a job into a set of smaller individual tasks that will make the process less overwhelming. You know how to find jobs that are advertised online and jobs that aren't. You know the importance of creating a killer resume, a cover letter that will place get your resume to the top of the application pile, and the importance of modifying your resume for each job you're applying for. You should understand the importance of having an online presence and a personal brand with a portfolio, a personal web page, blogs, and a LinkedIn profile.

Also, you should be well aware of the importance of networking and how to overcome the obstacles of networking if you are reluctant to do so. And you now know the importance of promoting yourself, establishing your own personal brand, and developing an attitude that attracts success. If you're shy or known to be afflicted by social anxiety, you should now have some tips at your fingertips to minimize those afflictions. You'll know how not to sabotage your efforts to get a job. You'll also know how to make a great first impression in an interview, standing out in a competitive market. And you now know what common questions you might expect during an interview. If you're changing careers, you now have some recommendations on how to turn that into a smooth transition. And you have tips on how

Job Search

to negotiate the salary you deserve in your new or current job. And you now know when and how to follow up on the applications you've sent to prospective employers.

Finding a great job is all about attitude and effort. If you can have a positive mindset and if you can do the work required to position yourself above other job candidates, you'll have a great chance to succeed in your job search.

Finding the job you desire can often be a lengthy or ongoing process and ultimately relies on decisions that are often beyond your control. But even though you can't control whether you get hired or not, you can control the process that allows you the best chance to get the job you're looking for. In order to be successful in your job search, you need to develop a plan and then work that plan.

As I've recommended multiple times in this book, in searching for a job you should always focus on the process, not the outcome. There may be times when you don't get the job you apply for, but don't let that discourage you. Focus on the process you're using to find the job, not on whether you get the job or not. You can control the process of your job search; you can't control the outcome. If you can do this, you'll have a great chance to get the job of your dreams.

Happy hunting!

You Are Hired! Job Interview Preparation

Stand Out From the Crowd, Know Exactly What to Answer, Show Them What You're Worth and Get Your Dream Job + Top Most Common Questions & Answers

Table of Contents

Introduction 99

Chapter 1—Score the Interview 103
   How to Land More Job Interviews Immediately. 103
   Tips for Building a Resume that Can Get You Hired. 107
   Cover Letters: Why You Need One and How to Make Yours Irresistible. 110

Chapter 2—Dress to Conquer 114
   What to Wear if You're a Man. 114
   What to Wear if You're a Woman. 117
   Six Things You Should Not Wear to an Interview. 119
   The Truth About Tattoos and Piercings. 121

Chapter 3—Prepare Like a Boss 125
   How to Overcome Anxiety and Nervousness. 125
   Nine Things You Need to Research for Your Interview. 129
   Other Vital Ways to Prepare for Your Job Interview. 134

Chapter 4—Questions and Answers 139
   12 Common Interview Questions and How to Ace Them. 139
   Navigating Difficult Questions Like a Champion. 144

Chapter 5—Make a Great First Impression 150
   Eight Things You Must Do to Make a Killer First Impression ... 150
   How to Instantly Stand Out Among Other Candidates. 154
   Confident Body Language that Puts You Ahead of the Game. .. 157

Chapter 6—Pass with Flying Colors 160
   11 Things Your Prospective Employer Wants to Hear. 160

Eight Things You Won't Want to Say in a Job Interview. 161

10 Soft Skills and How to Demonstrate Them. 163

Chapter 7—Finishing Touches **168**

11 Great Questions to Ask the Hiring Manager. 168

An Essential Guide to Salary Negotiations. 171

What to Do When You Get a Question that Throws You Off-Guard. 174

Is It OK to Lie?; When Is It OK to Lie in an Interview? 175

Chapter 8—The Future is Waiting **179**

What to do after the job interview. 179

You Got the Job! Now what? 181

How to Transform a Rejection into Something Positive. 183

Conclusion **188**

Introduction

For most of us, we had to learn to crawl before we could learn to walk. The same goes with finding the job of your dreams. Before you can get the job you've always wanted, you'll have to get an interview for the job. And then you'll have to ace that interview, passing it with flying colors and positioning yourself above other candidates for the same job. Many great candidates have lost job opportunities because they either were not able to get interviews or they came up empty in the interviews they had. Maybe they didn't have a resume that stood out above other candidates. Maybe their cover letter was lacking. Maybe they didn't dress appropriately for the interview. Maybe they didn't prepare properly. Maybe they got stumped by a question in the interview or maybe they said something wrong. Maybe, maybe, maybe... In getting and then acing interviews, it's extremely important that you have a plan and a process which gives you the best chance possible to get the job you're looking for.

In this book, I'm going to give you the tools and techniques you'll need to score interviews for the jobs you're interested in. I'm also going to tell you the things you'll need to do in the interview itself, including how to prepare for questions, how to dress, how to navigate difficult questions, what questions to ask prospective employers, how to broach and negotiate salary, and what to do in following up after the interview. All in all, I'll tell you how to position yourself above other candidates who are applying for the same job.

My name is David Allen. I am a how-to-get-a-job expert. I have years of experience as a human resources director for multiple companies in different industries. I've also worked as a recruiter, recruiting people to fill various corporate job openings. And finally, I also work as a career counselor, helping people find optimum career paths or jobs that will enable them to live happy, healthy, and successful lives. Over the years, I've noted that so many people are unable to get the jobs they want, simply because they don't know how to get interviews, how to prepare for interviews, or how to perform in the actual interview itself. Many of my clients who have had success based on the knowledge I've provided, have encouraged me to detail my knowledge in the form of a book. With this book, I've now done that, in the hopes that I'll be able to help a lot more people in their efforts to get the jobs they want.

If you can implement some of the tips and techniques I'm providing in this book, you'll enhance your chances of getting interviews for the jobs you're interested in and, subsequently, landing the jobs you really want. As a career counselor, I've worked with clients who had been trying for years to get the interviews or the jobs they were interested in. These clients came to me because they were not successful in their efforts and they wanted to know how they could improve their chances of securing the jobs they were looking for. In following some of the simple recommendations and steps I provided, these clients immediately found that they were having more success in getting interviews and in the results of those interviews. Many of these clients were unaware of what they were doing wrong, the things that made them unsuccessful in their efforts. With some simple tweaking, I was able to help these clients get the jobs they wanted.

Whether these clients were looking to find a job in which they made more money, find a job which utilized their talents more adequately, or find a job which had a better work environment, I was able to point them in the right direction and work with them in developing a plan or a process which enabled them to be successful in their pursuit of the job they wanted. Through the years, I've received emails, phone calls, and handwritten notes thanking me for my help in this process. Some of my clients have even told me that the information and advice I provided was life-altering. I sincerely hope that I can make the same impact on your job search and possibly even your career. I'd be delighted to receive a note from you someday soon telling me that in

Job Interview Preparation

this book I provided you with tips and techniques you used to land the job of your dreams.

If you'll read this short book and follow the tips and techniques I've provided, I'll assure you that you'll increase your chances to get job interviews and also increase the chances of getting the job itself. Before you can land the job you really want, you'll need to get the interview. Baby steps…you'll have to learn to crawl before you can learn to walk. And then once you get the interview, there are some surefire ways to ensure that you can be your best self in acing that interview. Getting a job is an activity that requires a plan and a process. Throughout this book, I will encourage you to develop a solid plan and then to focus more on the process of being your best self in trying to get the job you want instead of focusing on the results of your efforts. If you can develop a plan based on my recommendations and then work that plan, I'll assure you that you will enhance your chances of getting the job you really want.

I've read before that self-help or how-to books of this nature generally illicit two different types of calls to action: Some readers will tuck the knowledge that is offered into the remote regions of their memory banks, saying that they'll implement those ideas at a later date, whenever they get around to it. For the most part, these people are generally unsuccessful in their efforts, as "life happens"/time passes and they never get around to implementing the plan they said they would someday implement. The other type of reader is the type who will take the information gained and implement it immediately. I only hope that you are this type of reader, as these are the people who are much more likely to be successful in their efforts. If you'll implement immediately the tips in this book which are appropriate to you, you'll be much more likely to be successful in landing interviews and jobs. No, I can't guarantee that you'll get the job you're interested in, but I will guarantee that you'll have a much better chance to do so. Again, the key will be to focus on the process of getting interviews and jobs as compared to the results.

The tips and techniques in this book have been proven to be successful. If you will take the time to read this short book and then implement a plan based on the information the book provides, you'll increase your chances to get the interviews and the jobs you really want. Each chapter of this book has specific tips and techniques which can help you be successful in your job-hunting efforts. So, that being said, "Let's get after it"!

Job Interview Preparation

Chapter 1—Score the Interview

Looking for a job can be a daunting task. It can be tedious, stressful, and disappointing. But, by breaking this down into individual tasks, you can make substantial progress in just a short amount of time. As mentioned before, you won't be able to get a job unless you get an interview first. With this in mind, this chapter outlines the best ways to ensure that you get interviews.

How to Land More Job Interviews Immediately.

Whenever you try to secure an interview with a prospective employer, it's extremely important for you to keep in mind that in, in almost all instances, you'll be one of multiple people applying for that job. With this in mind, you're going to have to make sure that you stand out from other applicants.

First of all, you should determine exactly what kind of position you want to apply for and also, if possible, what kind of company you would like to work for. As an example, if you have a marketing background and you are interested in a marketing job, I would suggest that you narrow your search within those parameters. A client of mine, who was looking to make a job change, had a background in restaurant marketing for two different franchised restaurant chains. He enjoyed different aspects of both these jobs, however he had grown stagnant with the restaurant company he was working for. So, in realizing that he enjoyed working in the restaurant and hospitality industry and also realizing that companies within the restaurant industry would value his experience, my client opted to look for a job within the restaurant industry. To narrow the field even further, he realized that his experience of working for a franchised company would be particularly attractive to another franchised restaurant company.

Job Interview Preparation

So, he targeted restaurant companies in his job search and narrowed the field even more by selecting some franchised restaurant companies in his search. He was fully aware of the things he could bring to the table for a restaurant company or a franchised company that other applicants might not be able to offer. So, instead of applying to be a marketing person in a tech company or an architectural company in which he had no experience (and not much interest), my client decided to target franchised restaurant groups. Also, it should be noted that he targeted a few companies which consisted mostly of company-owned restaurants and a few companies in other franchised industries, including a franchised health club chain and a franchised print shop chain. In other words, my client took a personal inventory of his experience and his likes and then used that information to determine the types of companies to which he wanted to submit applications.

Once he did that, he adjusted his resume to fit that particular industry or those particular companies. For instance, with the franchised health club chains, he mentioned early in his resume that he had considerable experience in working with franchisees from all different areas of the country. He was aware that the franchised health club chain, which had started in one area of the company, was now expanding to other areas of the country and he he realized that this experience of working with franchisees in different areas of the country would likely be particularly valuable to the company he was interested in working for. Although I'll give you additional tips on how to develop a resume that stands out later in this chapter, I'll tell you now that it will be very important for you to continue to tweak and adjust your resume based on the companies you are sending it to. No, you can't just develop one resume, make 100 copies of that resume, and then send it out for every job you're interested in. If you want to be successful in getting interviews, you'll need to continue to fine tune your resume for each job you're applying for.

Another way to ensure that you'll land more interviews will be to prepare and update your personal marketing materials before you even begin sending out resumes. Do you have business cards that you can hand out at networking events or any time you meet someone who could be a possible job source for you? Do you have a LinkedIn profile? (If not, you should have one.) If you have a LinkedIn profile, have you updated that profile? Are you present on social media platforms such as Facebook, Instagram, and Twitter? If so, do those sites convey you as a person who would be an asset to a company that is hiring? Is there any negative information on those sites that might impact your chances of landing a job? If so, can that information be deleted? Or, if it can't be deleted, is it something that can be addressed or justified if a prospective employer asks you about it in an interview? Do you have your own personal web page or a blog site? If not, are these things that might help you secure a new job? If you have a personal web site or blog site, make sure those sites reflect a positive image to a prospective employer.

In trying to determine which companies might be hiring, it's important to note that an extraordinary number of job openings are not advertised. I've seen research which shows that over 90% of all jobs are not advertised. Although this seems a bit high to me, the importance of the thought should not be lost…most job openings are not posted. With this in mind, I'll tell you that even though it is certainly important for you to search job boards when looking for jobs, you should never stop there. Companies often don't post jobs on job boards because they don't want to be swamped with resumes, many from candidates who are not qualified. Other companies prefer to solicit their own candidates through internal postings or by searching through resumes on LinkedIn or other job platforms and then inviting qualified candidates to interview. Other companies will hire recruiters, often referred to as headhunters, to bring candidates to them.

And finally, in your efforts to find out about job openings and secure interviews, I strongly encourage you to network. Network, network, network. Even if you don't participate regularly with any organized networking groups or professional organizations, I encourage you to have a "networking mindset", which means that you are consistently telling people about the positions you are looking for. I always like to tell the following story, which comes from a client of mine. She was looking for an accounting job in a specific major retail store chain. Her research had told her that this company was a great company to work for, however she had no contacts there and no way to get her foot in the door for an interview. She made a habit of telling most of the people she knew that she was interested in getting an interview with this particular company she had targeted. Eventually, when she was at her hair salon, she mentioned this to her hair stylist. Sure enough, the stylist responded that her brother-in-law was one of the head accounting people in the company my client was interested in. The stylist asked for a business card to pass along to her brother-in-law and my client gladly complied. Less than a week later, my client got a call from the stylist's brother-in-law. This call resulted in an interview. After a series of interviews, my client is now happily employed at the company she targeted. The morals of the story: Network; spread the word; don't ignore any possible sources. Who would have thought that a contact with a hair stylist could lead to an accounting position in a major retail chain? But it did. If you've targeted specific companies you want to work for, don't hesitate to ask anyone you know if they know anyone inside that company.

Another obvious approach to get interviews with a targeted company is to simply find out who the hiring manager is for that company and then call them. If you're lucky, you'll be able to talk directly to the hiring manager. If not, you may have to go through the gatekeeper or the secretary to find out if there are any current openings. Even if there are no current openings, I encourage you to send a follow up note directly to the hiring manager and express your interest in working for the company. Ask them to contact you whenever there is an opening. And one other footnote: If there is a gatekeeper and you have a feeling that the gatekeeper is not forwarding your information to the hiring manager, you might try to call just before or soon after normal work hours before the gatekeeper arrives or before he or she leaves for the day. Many of my clients have found those before or after regular work hours to be the best times to reach hiring managers directly by phone.

And, whether you can't get past the gatekeeper or if the hiring manager tells you that there are no current openings, it's always important for you to follow up in some way, shape, or form, whether that's with a phone call or a personal "thanks for your time" note. Be persistent without becoming a nuisance. Your goal in any follow up should be to convey that you have sincere interest in interviewing with or working for that company and for you to create top-of-the-mind awareness as a possible candidate. This small gesture of following up can sometimes place you above other candidates when a job comes open.

Tips for Building a Resume that Can Get You Hired.

Your resume is likely to be a key element in determining whether or not you are able to secure an interview. In developing your resume, you should remember that it will often be compared side-by-side with the resumes of other candidates. With this in mind, you'll want to make sure that your resume stands out compared to these other resumes. Here are some basic tips which you can use in building a resume that will get you hired:

Before you build your own resume, you should review other sample resumes, which are very easy to find on the internet. If you are looking for a job in specific industries, I suggest that you also search industry-specific resumes to see what other people are doing in the same industry. (LinkedIn is a great place to view resumes of people within specific industries.)

After you've reviewed various sample resumes, you should then find out what standard resume templates are available. You can find resume templates by simply searching "free resume templates" on the internet. Also, as many of us have Microsoft Word, that software program has free resume templates available. Take a look at some of these templates and determine a template that will work for you.

One of the keys in developing any resume is to make it easy to read. This means that you should use a simple type style, such as Helvetica, Times Roman, Arial, or Calibri. Nothing too fancy. Type size should generally be 10 or 12 point type, nothing smaller. You should limit your resume to one or two pages, nothing longer. If you want to use color highlights and bold or italic type in some areas, you should feel free to do so, as long as you don't overuse these functions. I've received resumes before that were loaded with bold, capital letters, sometimes color-highlighted and underlined. In viewing these resumes, I've often felt that the sender is screaming at me, trying way too hard to get my attention.

In drafting your resume, you should remember that in most instances you'll be tweaking or adjusting each resume you send, depending on the job you are applying for. In customizing your resume for a particular job application, I encourage you to read the posting or description for the job and then make note of the keywords within that posting. Those keywords should give you a good idea as to what qualities or experience the employer is looking for in the employee they hire. You should then try to work some of these keywords into both your resume and your cover letter, without being too obvious. Also, if you are applying for a job at a larger company or a branch of a larger company, you should remember that many companies are now using a software bot to initially read your resume before it is passed along to a human. Some of these software bots are programmed to search for keywords. That's another reason why it's important to include the employer's keywords in your resume.

Job Interview Preparation

In listing information on your resume, also make a point to list important and relevant information first. In other words, if you're 40 years old, over 20 years removed from high school, you should not list your high school accomplishments near the top of your resume. List the experience, the accomplishments, the information which is most relevant to the job you are applying for. In listing your accomplishments, list numbers whenever possible. For example, if you had experience as a salesperson previously, instead of just saying that you were the salesperson for the North Central region, you might point out that you increased sales by 32% over the period of two years in the North Central region you were responsible for. Or, if you were on a salesforce of 13 people, and were the company's salesperson of the year, you need to make note of that. The more specific you can be, the more your talents and accomplishments will resonate with the prospective employer.

Also, you should use active/powerful language whenever possible to outline your achievements. Words like "achieved", "earned", "accomplished", and "completed" are examples of power words which can be used to outline the achievements and accomplishments in your resume.

And make sure that your resume includes your contact information. (Phone number, email address, etc.) It's going to be hard for you to get an interview if the prospective employer doesn't know how to get a hold of you.

And finally, please proofread your resume and cover letter multiple times to make sure there are no typographical errors or other errors. I strongly suggest that you have other people check your resume for errors. Errors, especially typos, are totally unacceptable on resumes and I know hiring managers who will discard any resumes that have obvious errors. The feeling is that if you can't pay attention to detail with a resume or cover letter, then you might not be able to pay attention to detail in the job the employer is hiring for. If you don't know anyone who is capable of proofreading your resume and cover letter and if you can't do it yourself, then I suggest that you hire a freelance proofreader to do that for you. Upwork is a freelance site in which you would be able to hire a proofreader, for maybe $5 to $10. Fiverr is another company that is a platform for freelancers, including proofreaders.

Cover Letters: Why You Need One and How to Make Yours Irresistible.

Whereas resumes should contain "just the facts", cover letters offer you additional opportunities to make a "pitch" for the job. Cover letters allow you to expand on some of the facts you listed on your resume. They allow you the opportunity to express your sincere interest in the job opening and explain why you are a good fit for the job. Also, cover letters allow you to showcase some of your personality and to establish yourself as someone who stands out above the other candidates applying for the same job.

Some job applicants make the major mistake of ignoring the importance of the cover letter, thinking that the hiring manager won't take the time to read it. I can unequivocally tell you that cover letters do get read by prospective employers and you should never ignore their importance. You should compose a fresh cover letter for each job you apply for.

Here are some tips to consider in writing those cover letters:

First of all, you need to identify the person you are sending the cover letter to and list their name in the salutation of the letter. Letters addressed "To Whom it May Concern" or "Hiring Manager" are not going to cut it. Get the name and the correct spelling of the person who is doing the hiring, even if you have to make a phone call to get this information. If, by chance, you're not able to get a name for whatever reason, you should at least get the title of the person who is doing the hiring. (i.e.—Director of Marketing, Human Resources Director, Accounting Manager, etc.)

As you write your cover letter, make sure you go beyond your resume. If you're just going to repeat all of the information that is on your resume, then you're diminishing the purpose of the cover letter. If there's anything on your resume that you'd like to expand upon, the cover letter offers you the opportunity to do so. Although you won't want to take up your entire cover letter in expanding upon something on your resume, the cover letter allows you a brief opportunity to do that.

It will help if you can come up with a great opening line for your letter. Whether you have a great opening line or not, early in your cover letter you should cover why you think you are a good fit for the job which is open. As an example, here is an opening line from someone who is applying for a management position in a Barnes & Noble bookstore. "I was excited to find that you have an opening for a management position at Barnes & Noble. I've been a fan and loyal customer of Barnes & Noble for many years now and, with my previous management experience, I feel that I can bring a lot to the table as a Barnes & Noble manager." In this opening line, you'll note that the applicant expresses their interest and enthusiasm for the job that is open. They also establish themselves as someone who is familiar with the company and loves the concept. (It's hard to quickly dismiss someone who is a loyal customer, right?) And then, the applicant highlights that they have management experience and notes that she thinks she can become a valuable part of the Barnes & Noble team. And, she does that with a casual tone, without being ridiculously formal. In two sentences, she's accomplished a lot.

When you are writing your cover letter, it's important that you are aware of the keywords which the prospective employer has used in their job post. In the Barnes & Noble job post, the company had stated that it was looking for someone with management experience. As a result, the applicant was quick to mention her management experience in her cover letter. Another example would be if a prospective employer says they are looking to hire a committed employee who can be a valuable part of the team. The keywords here are "committed" and "team". With this in mind, your cover letter might mention that you are a hard worker and that you work well with others as part of a team. In reiterating the keywords from the job posting, you'll be reinforcing that you are a good fit for their job.

In your letter, you should explain why you are a better fit than any other people who are applying for the same position. If you're short on the experience or credentials they're asking for, then you're going to have to emphasize less tangible assets, such as positive attitude, work ethic, employee loyalty, etc. In doing this, I recommend that you do not point out or mention your lack of experience or credentials. Let the prospective employer discover this themselves. Instead of saying, "Although I don't have much experience….", you should say, "I am willing to work hard to become an invaluable member of the team" or "As my previous supervisor would tell you, I have a positive 'can do' attitude, I am a loyal employee, and I work well with others." Again, don't apologize for lack of experience or credentials. Identify the keywords in the job posting which apply to you and then highlight the attributes you have that correspond with those keywords. (If you don't fit with any or many of the keywords in the job posting, you may not be a good fit for the job.)

Also, in creating your cover letter, please remember to emphasize "what you can do for the company" instead of "what the company can do for you." The hiring manager already knows what the company can do for you. Your approach should be to tell them what you can bring to the table if they hire you. Hiring managers don't want to hear that their jobs will feed your family, allow you to get the sports car you've always wanted, or place you on the career path you want to be on. Instead, you need to highlight what you can do for them and their company.

Job Interview Preparation

And, similar to the recommendations made for resumes, if you get a chance to use numbers to illustrate your past successes, you should do so. (i.e.—"As sales manager for the Northeast Region, I increased sales by 65% the first year and 32% the second year.") Again, remember that hiring managers like numbers to illustrate past successes. Tangible assets are usually preferred over intangible assets in resumes and cover letters.

Cover letters also offer you the opportunities for testimonials, although you should again remember that cover letter space is somewhat limited. If you get the chance to use a testimonial, you should do so. (i.e.—"My supervisor told me that I had performed like a superhero in organizing that event", "One of my customers told me that the assistance I provided had 'saved the day' ", "I consistently received top reviews for my ability to guide our customer service team", etc.)

I strongly recommend that you keep your cover letters to one page only. And even though you should have listed your contact info on your resume, you should list the same contact info on your cover letter in case the resume and cover letter end up getting separated.

And, finally, another reminder for you to make sure that you have proofread your cover letter before sending. Typographical or grammatical errors could well eliminate you from consideration. If at all possible, use an additional set of eyes to proof your cover letter and your resume. Enlist the services of someone who is good at proofreading.

Chapter 2—Dress to Conquer

Okay, you've landed a face-to-face interview. What's next? Well, one of the things that is often overlooked is the decision on how to dress and what to wear for the interview. Although I've never been a "What to wear? What to wear?" person, as a career counselor I've seen applicants lose job opportunities based on the way they've dressed for an interview. With this in mind, here are some recommendations and suggestions on how you should dress for your interview.

What to Wear if You're a Man.

Unlike women's interview attire, men's interview attire is relatively straightforward. I always tell my male clients that, as an interviewee, their goal in regards to their attire should be not to stand out in an interview. If a man is standing out in an interview by the way he is dressed, it may well mean that the interviewer viewed his attire negatively. As a male, even though you certainly want to dress for success in any interview, your goal should simply be to fit in from an attire standpoint. Your ultimate goal should be to get the job based on what you say in the interview and what you have to offer, not on how you are dressed. If you think that a hiring manager is going to hire you based on the way you're dressed, unless you're applying for a job in the fashion industry, you're probably focusing on the wrong area. That being said, you can't disregard the importance of dressing for success and making a good impression based on the way you dress.

I'll never forget my first interview out of college. As a fresh-faced 21-year-old, I had the opportunity to interview for a public relations job with a major restaurant chain. At that time, many years ago, the company had all five selected candidates sit in the lobby at the same time as we waited to be interviewed. In sitting in the lobby with the

Job Interview Preparation

other four applicants, it was immediately apparent that I was the kid fresh out of college and the other four candidates, also males, were older and experienced. I wore my only suit, my baby blue "interview suit", and a pair of spongy-soled dress shoes. The other candidates all wore more traditional attire, darker suits and more traditional shoes, including wingtips and penny loafers. I knew immediately that my interview attire would make me stand out from the other candidates, and not in a good way. But then again, I was less than a couple weeks out of college and I didn't know any better. I was fortunate enough to get invited back for a second interview for a job I really wanted. Again, as a kid right out of college, I was accustomed to wearing jeans and t-shirts every day and my "baby blue" interview suit was the only suit I owned. As I didn't want to wear the same suit to the second interview and I had no money to buy another suit, I borrowed my college roommate's suit for the second interview. Thankfully, we were about the same size; thankfully, I was offered the job despite my wardrobe deficiency. But I learned a lesson from that, and I made sure that I was dressed more appropriately for my subsequent interviews with other companies years later.

In determining what to wear for an interview, it will be helpful if you know what the dress code or dress mode is for the company you're interviewing with. Not all companies dress alike and you'll find that employees for a startup company are likely to dress different than employees who work for a corporate law firm. If you're not sure of what a particular company's dress code is, and you really want to make sure that you fit in when you are there for your interview, there's no harm in calling the receptionist at that company to find out how most people dress. I've even had clients who have gone to the company they were scheduled to interview with and, days before the interview, scoped out how employees are dressed with a reconnaissance mission in the parking lot. Although I think this is a bit drastic, it does point out that it's important for you not to look too out of place with what you wear for your interview.

Job Interview Preparation

Hopefully, you'll know something about the company you sent your resume to and you'll have a feel for what kind of business they're in and how they might dress. If you're interviewing for the position of a golf pro or a landscaper, you can obviously dress very casual for your interview. As a matter of fact, you'd probably surely lose points if you showed up in a coat and tie. But for most other jobs, you may want to determine if the company you're interviewing with has business casual or business formal. The basic difference between these two modes of attire primarily deals with whether you should wear a tie or not, but also may deal with whether you should plan to wear a suitcoat or not.

Either way, I always tell my male clients that, if they're going to wear a coat, a khaki coat or camel-color coat is preferred over a darker coat. I tell clients not to dress like they would dress for going to a funeral. Pinstripe suits may be too formal, depending on the job you're applying for. Navy blazers may be more appropriate. Pants should obviously be coordinated with the coat. Navy, khaki, or even grey slacks are standard for most interviews. Whether you wear a tie or not may depend on whether you're going for the business casual or business formal look. Business casual is often without a tie, while business formal usually includes a tie.

If you're trying to straddle the line between business casual and business formal, a button-down shirt layered with a sweater is often acceptable attire, unless the sweater is the sweater you bought for an ugly sweater party. Again, whether you wear a tie will depend on whether you are going for the business casual or business formal look.

With your tie choice, you should select a tie that's not too bizarre, but it doesn't have to be boring either.

In choosing a button-down shirt, I recommend that you choose a solid color shirt or a pinstripe shirt, something that works with the other items you're going to wear and something that won't detract from the overall look. I recommend that you choose a long sleeve button-down over a short sleeve button-down, only because I know some people who are adverse to short sleeve button-downs for men.

Based on the rest of your interview attire, you should choose a nice pair of conservative shoes that works with the outfit. Nothing wrong with wearing brown shoes in conjunction with a business casual or business formal look. And make sure that your shoes are polished, certainly not scuffed. Also, a leather belt and conservative dark socks are normal interview attire for men, although with some of the unique and colorful sock designs today, patterned socks might work also.

And if you're a heavy jewelry wearer, go light on the jewelry unless you're applying for a job as a rap music producer. Joke. The same goes for cologne or after-shave. Go without or go very light.

And make sure your fingernails are clean and properly manicured.

What to Wear if You're a Woman.

It shouldn't surprise anyone when I say that deciding what to wear for an interview is often more complicated for women than it is for men. Although I'm going to spend more time on women's attire than I did for men's attire, I want to caution women and tell them not to overthink the attire you decide to wear to an interview. Although the way you dress in an interview is certainly important, it is still secondary compared to preparing for the verbal parts of the interview itself.

How you dress for an interview will again depend on the type of company you're interviewing with. Dress codes for different companies can vary substantially. A startup company might allow jeans and tennis shoes, while a Fortune 500 Madison Avenue company might even discourage any attire that doesn't include a skirt and pantyhose. That's why it's important for you to find out what kind of dress code the company you're interviewing with has before you interview. Again, if you're not sure, you might simply call the company receptionist and ask about the dress code or standard attire. And, if you're still not sure, I would tell you that it's better to dress up instead of dressing down compared to the level of the employees there.

In most cases, I encourage women to dress conservatively. Nothing too flashy. Nothing too revealing in terms of top or skirt length. Normal conservative skirt length is just above or just below the knee. Select a conservative blouse or top that coordinates with your outfit.

Unlike men, accessories are more of a major factor for women. If you're a woman, you have to choose whether to wear jewelry or not. And, if you choose to wear jewelry, you'll have to choose what jewelry to wear. Also, you'll have to choose what bag to bring to an interview. In terms of jewelry, some people maintain that women should wear little or no jewelry to an interview. Either way, it's safe to say that you shouldn't overload the amount of jewelry you wear to an interview. I have a friend in the career counseling business who tells women that she would rather see them wear no jewelry at all instead of cheap jewelry. Also, in terms of the bag you choose to bring with you to an interview, the bag should be large enough to hold your resume and any corresponding paperwork, however it should not be one of those monstrous bags that we sometimes see. In my human resources days, I once had a woman that brought it bag so big into her interview that it took her at least five minutes to find her resume. In looking for her resume, she proceeded to empty her bag of its contents, piece by piece. By the time she finally located her resume, she could have had a garage sale with all the items she had placed on my desk, and, during that time, I had formed an opinion that she was disorganized. In other words, her chances of getting that job had ended even before the interview really got started.

Also, I encourage women to be cognizant of the amount of makeup and the perfume they wear. I would encourage women to go light on the makeup and to go without or go light on the perfume. It's important to remember that some people are allergic to perfumes and other people detest the heavy use of perfumes. With this in mind, the use of perfumes in an interview probably isn't a risk that's worth the reward.

Just as I advised men to make sure they had clean manicured nails, I encourage women to make sure their nails are presentable.

Clothes should be always be conservative, so as not to detract from the interview itself. The clothes themselves should be ironed and/or wrinkle-free. They should also be clean. No stains, holes, snags, or ragged edges. And beware of pet hair if you have a dog or cat.

Shoes should be polished and not scuffed. Whether you wear high heels or flats is up to you. Open-toe shoes are discouraged.

If you're going to a startup interview with a company that has a very casual dress code, jeans and tennis shoes may be OK, but the jeans should be clean and without holes and ragged seams. If you are interviewing with a company that has a very casual dress code, I strongly encourage you to make absolutely sure how casual it is before wearing jeans and tennis shoes to an interview. If you're wrong with that, your chance to get the job could be over before the interview starts. If you're not sure, then it's safer to dress up instead of taking the risk of dressing down.

Six Things You Should Not Wear to an Interview.

Although many of these things are common-sensical, there are some definite no-no's in what you should not wear or take to an interview.

1) Bright, flashy clothes. Try not to look like a decorated, walking Christmas tree. Stick with more conservative, solid colors. If you're going to wear a bright color, such as a bright red top, make sure that the rest of your outfit offsets or balances the bright colors you're

Job Interview Preparation

wearing. Again, the goal here is for you not to stand out for the clothes you are wearing. You simply want to look polished and professional.

2) Scuffed, dirty, or outdated shoes. This tip applies to both men and women. You'd be surprised at how many people pay close attention to shoes and I'm presuming that hiring managers are included.

3) Too much jewelry or too many accessories. If you're a man, take off the bling or tuck it inside your shirt. If you're a woman, no large dangling earrings. And if you wear funky eyeglasses, go back to your more conventional and conservative design, at least for purposes of the interview.

4) Outlandish ties, scarves, socks. This applies particularly to men, but also to women who accessorize with scarves. If you're a man, don't try to be the funny guy with an outlandish tie or socks. You're not there to enhance your future as a standup comic. If you are a bow tie wearer, you might consider a more conventional necktie. Although I think bow ties can be quite fashionable, you should know that some people still have an aversion to them.

5) Heavy makeup; heavy perfume or colon. Instead of wearing heavy makeup, or heavy perfume or cologne, I'd recommend that you either go light or go without. Some people are allergic to perfumes or colognes; other people are very sensitive to scents. You never know if one of the people you meet in an interview with be of the same kind. Also, go light on the makeup. Don't overdo it. Avoid bright red lipstick and dark eyeshadow. A light coat of mascara, a touch of powder, and some tinted lip balm are probably OK, but don't overdo it.

6) Outdated or worn bags, portfolios, briefcases. Some people totally forget about the bags or briefcases they use to carry their resume or interview paperwork. Make sure that the vessel you're using is presentable and professional, and conveys the image you want to present to your prospective employer. If you're a woman with a bag, choose a smaller size bag and minimize the contents so you can easily find the paperwork you'll need during your interview. And always bring a pen.

Again, with any of these recommendations, you should know that they're not set in concrete. I always encourage people to be who they are and to dress accordingly. However, in choosing what to wear and how you want to look for an interview, always keep in mind the person or persons you might be meeting during the interview and consider what kind of impression you're making with the way you're dressed or accessorized.

The Truth About Tattoos and Piercings.

So, you have some tattoos or some piercings. Well, you're certainly not alone. Almost 30% of Americans have tattoos and half of all millennials have tattoos. That being said, you're probably aware that some people still have some biases or negative feelings about tattoos and piercings and, with this in mind, you may have to decide how you're going to handle that going into an interview.

First of all, let me point out that with some jobs and some employers, it's not going to matter at all whether you have tattoos or piercings. However, some other companies may even have company policies in place regarding tattoos and piercings.

Before we discuss how you should handle tattoos and piercings going into an interview, I'd like to provide you with some additional information which may help you in your decision on how to handle. A popular survey site recently revealed the results of a survey they did regarding tattoos and piercing. They asked respondents if they felt that tattoos and piercings hurt an applicant's chances of getting a job. 76% of respondents felt that tattoos and piercings did indeed hurt an applicant's chances in getting a job. Along the same lines, over 37% of the people surveyed said that they felt that employees with tattoos and piercings reflected poorly on their employers. 42% thought that visible tattoos were inappropriate at work; 55% felt that piercings were inappropriate at work.

In looking at these survey results, there's no denying that there is still a lot of bias against tattoos and piercings, whether that's fair or not. It should be pointed out that peoples' age is a significant factor in how tattoos and piercings are perceived. As you might guess, older age groups have a more negative perception of tattoos and piercings; younger age groups are more accepting.

People who have negative perceptions of tattoos and piercings are prone to think that people who have these tattoos and piercings are, among other things, less intelligent (27% of respondents thought that people with tattoos and piercings were less intelligent than people without tattoos and piercings, less attractive (45%), and more rebellious (50%). Unfortunately, the perceptions of women with tattoos and piercings are even worse than the perceptions of men. Whereas some people perceive men with tattoos as being more masculine, more dominant, and more aggressive, women with tattoos are perceived to be less honest, less motivated, less generous, and less creative, among other things. Those negative perceptions are most certainly an unfair burden to bear for a qualified candidate. I list these seemingly unfair assumptions only so you can see what perceptions you're dealing with if you're someone that has tattoos or piercings. You may be a perfectly qualified candidate for a job position, but you may be stigmatized or categorized because you have tattoos or piercings.

Job Interview Preparation

In deciding whether you should hide your tattoos in an interview or to allow them to be seen, here are some possible factors:

1) Consider the industry and the position you are applying to. If you're going to be face to face with customers in that position, you may well have to cover your tattoos and ditch the piercings. Positions such as face-to-face customer service representatives, retail sales people, and bank tellers are all positions in which you're going to be working with the public on an ongoing basis and, as a result, your employer may not allow you to have your tattoos and piercings visible.

2) Research and consider the company culture. As mentioned before, some companies even have company policies against tattoos and piercings. If they do, you're going to have to make a decision on how important it is for you to exhibit your tattoos and piercings, both in the interview and on the job, if you get the job. If you're adamant about not hiding your tattoos or piercings and if the company you're interested in has a policy against tattoos or piercings, you should know that this may impact your interest in working for that company or their interest in hiring you. In other words, it may be a dealbreaker.

3) Hide them in the interview and then ask later. If you're not sure what the company stance is on tattoos and piercings going into the interview, it's probably best to hide them (if possible) for the interview. If you have tattoos on your arms that can be simply covered with a long sleeve shirt, then cover them for the interview and if it appears that the interviewer has further interest in you as a candidate, you can always ask him or her if there is a company policy regarding tattoos or piercings. If you have tattoos that can't be covered, such as tattoos on your fingers or the side of your face, you'll certainly have to broach that in the interview as it's unlikely that you'll be able to cover your face or your hands in most of the jobs you apply for. Whenever I discuss tattoos in this chapter, please know that I'm

Job Interview Preparation

presuming that the tattoos you have are not offensive. If you have tattoos that are going to be offensive to co-workers or customers, that's a whole different scenario and you may well find that those tattoos may prohibit you from getting a job and you may have to have them altered or removed before you can get a job.

4) Don't let your tattoos or piercings be a distraction in an interview. When you interview for a job, you're hopefully going to want your talents and abilities to be the main determinants as to whether you get the job or not. With this in mind, you won't want your tattoos or piercings to be a distraction in the interview. Getting a great job can be difficult enough without having your tattoos detract from the reasons you're the right person for the job.

In summary, please know that I always encourage people to be themselves when they interview. I can't tell you whether you should hide your tattoos or piercings or whether you should allow them to be visible. You'll have to make that decision yourself. However, I did want to arm you with some information and remind you that some people still have a bias against and a negative perception of tattoos and piercings. Depending on the company you're interviewing with and the position you're applying for, you'll have to determine whether exhibiting your tattoos and piercings will inhibit your chances to get a job that you're interested in. And you'll also have to determine whether the tattoos or piercings would prohibit you from doing the job itself. If the company has a policy against visible tattoos, are you going to be willing to cover your tattoos every day? If you're really interested in the job and you don't have a problem with hiding your tattoos and dissing your piercings, then I recommend that you hide them during the interview. Then if you and the prospective employer have further interest in the opening, you should find out what company policy is toward displaying these markings.

Chapter 3—Prepare Like a Boss

In preparing for an interview, it's important that you prepare for that interview as much as possible. Preparation is a great way for you to overcome any anxiety you might have going into an interview. If you've prepared properly, you'll give yourself the best chance to land the job.

How to Overcome Anxiety and Nervousness.

First of all, let me tell you that it's normal to feel nervous or have some butterflies going into an interview. After all, that interview may well hold the key to your future and you shouldn't ignore the fact that it could provide the next step for you in your career or your livelihood. So, don't let the fact that you have some anxiety alarm you. It's natural.

With this section of the book, I'm going to give you some suggestions on how you can conquer your anxiety as you prepare for the interview and also in the interview itself. Most of my suggestions will revolve around preparation. If you prepare adequately for your interview, you'll give yourself the chance to ace the interview and land a job offer.

My first recommendations involve eating and sleeping. You should make sure you're well rested before you head into an interview. Get a good night of sleep. Also, lay off the caffeine, as it will only increase your anxiety. No caffeinated coffee, no caffeinated soft drinks. And, obviously don't drink alcohol before an interview. This includes not drinking too much the night before the interview. I also suggest that you eat something or have a light snack before going into an interview. I had a client who went into an interview with an empty stomach and, as a result, her stomach was growling loudly throughout the interview.

Job Interview Preparation

She was so embarrassed that she couldn't focus on the interview. In a similar horror story, I had another client who ate a greasy meal before his interview and, as a result, he had to ask to use the restroom in the middle of the interview. Along the same lines, I've also had clients tell me that the heavy meals they ate before interviews made them sleepy during the interview. So, bottom line is that you need to pay attention to what you eat and drink prior to an interview.

Another way to reduce anxiety for your interview will be to make sure you arrive on time, presuming it's a face-to-face interview. If you arrive just before an interview, you may increase your anxiety. If you arrive late, you may be eliminated from the job opportunity before the interview even starts. And, if by chance, you find out that you're going to be late for the interview, you need to call the person you were supposed to meet with and tell them you will be late. You'd be surprised how many people show up late for interviews without informing the person they're meeting with. If you're not exactly sure how to get to the location where the interview is being held, make sure you find out how to get there. Use Mapquest or one of the other internet sites to get driving directions or use the GPS system on your phone to guide you and make sure that you allow time for possible traffic delays. If weather is an issue and is creating poor driving conditions, I suggest that you contact the interviewer before you even set out to drive there; then keep them posted on your progress if anything changes as you work your way toward their location. If the job is important enough to you, and the location isn't too far from you, I've had clients who've made trial runs in the days before the interview. But if you're doing a trial run, make sure you're accounting for the time of day and the different traffic levels during the time of day. I've had clients who did their trial runs during non-business hours and then when they travelled to their interview location during rush hour, the transit time was much longer and they found they hadn't allowed enough transit time.

Job Interview Preparation

Another way to reduce interview anxiety is to plan what you're going to wear ahead of time, at least a day ahead of time. I've had clients who have waiting until the morning of the interview to decide what they were going to wear for an interview, only to find that the suitcoat they planned to wear had a stain on it or was loaded with pet hair, the shirt or blouse they planned to wear had more wrinkles than a Shar-pei, or the shoes they planned to wear needed polishing. If you're running around trying to plan your wardrobe on the day of the interview, you'll most certainly be increasing your anxiety.

It's also important that you do your homework regarding the company you're interviewing with, especially if you're not familiar with them. The internet offers all of us the chance to research companies from our living rooms. If you haven't visited the web site of the company you'll be interviewing with, you need to do so. Also, please use Google or another search engine to see if there are any recent news articles that provide information on the company. I had a client who, when researching the company she was going to interview with, found out that the company was having some serious financial issues that she hadn't been aware of. Although this information didn't discourage her from proceeding with the interview, it certainly gave her some questions to ask during the interview. Another way to learn about the companies you are interviewing with is to solicit personal information. Do you know someone who works for that company or worked for them in the past? Do you know someone who works for a competitor of the company you're interviewing with? In soliciting personal information and even with searching for information on the internet, I always caution people to take their findings with "a grain of salt". The information you receive could be inaccurate or tainted, but nevertheless it should at least give you some food for thought and possibly some information or questions that will help you in your interview.

Another way for you to reduce your anxiety is to prepare for the actual interview itself. First, make sure you have all the necessary materials to take with you to the interview: resume, copy of your cover letter, reference list, portfolio with samples of your work, certifications, licenses, business cards, and certainly a pen and notepad. Again, pay attention to detail with the materials you gather. No coffee or soda stains on your resume, no pens that you or your dog have chewed, etc. You get the picture.

Also, in preparing for an interview, you can reduce your anxiety by determining some of the questions you want to ask before the interview. If you think there's a chance you won't remember the questions you want to ask, write them down on a sheet of paper and take that with you to the interview.

Do you have a friend or relative who you can practice the interview with? If so, you might find that conducting a mock interview will be very helpful. Give your friend some questions to ask you based on the questions you think you'll be asked during the interview itself. People who do mock interviews prior to their actual interviews seem to benefit immensely from the practice of formulating and giving answers to possible questions. There's no doubt that this practice boosts confidence heading into the interview.

As you head into an interview, you may find it beneficial to "step outside yourself" and the thoughts of the interview itself. Some people find this extremely helpful, as they relish every part of the interview process. They greet and engage the receptionist, they say a brief hello to any people they pass along the way to the interview room, they ask the interviewer how his or her day is going, they focus on remembering the names of the people they meet, they focus on a firm handshake and eye-to-eye contact, etc. In other words, they break each part of the interview process into a separate event and, as a result, it's much easier for them to relax and cast off any anxiety they might be feeling.

In the interview itself, I always encourage people to "slow down". When we get anxious, we tend to rush things and that can lead to undesirable results. I have a friend who is a youth basketball coach and during big moments of the games when his players may be experiencing anxiety, he always tells them to slow down. The same goes with interviews. If you have anxiety and the interviewer asks you a question, instead of blurting out the answer, slow down and take some time and think about how you want to answer the question. That should be helpful in reducing your anxiety.

Along the same lines, you should note that some interviewers will try to catch applicants off-guard by grilling them or interrogating them. For applicants with anxiety, this can really throw them off track. If this happens to you, you should understand why the interviewer may be doing this and you should also understand that he or she is probably using the same tack with other candidates. Interviewers will sometimes grill candidates in order to find out how the candidate will react to stress. If you know in advance that this is an approach used by some interviewers, you'll feel a lot less anxiety knowing what the motivation is and knowing that all candidates are probably being handled in the same manner.

And finally, another way to reduce your anxiety in an interview is to ask the interviewer some questions and let them answer. "Throw the ball in their court", in other words. Hopefully, you'll have some questions prepared in advance and you'll also be able to formulate other questions throughout the interview. You'll find that you'll have a much better chance to land the job if you can turn the interview from a monologue into a two-way conversation. Not only will you have less anxiety, you may well find that the interview feels much better about the interview if it is a conversation instead of an interrogation.

Nine Things You Need to Research for Your Interview.

Research is a huge part of the preparation for any interview. If you want to give yourself the best chance to land the job, you'll make sure

Job Interview Preparation

that you've researched the job you're applying for and the corresponding company.

1) About the Company. You'd be surprised how many job applicants don't know much about the company they're interviewing with. When the interviewer asks what you know about the company and you respond, "Well, my brother-in-law told me it's a great place to work", that's not going to cut it. You'll actually have to know something more about the company you're hoping to work for. The internet and Google make it very easy for job applicants to research companies. Almost all companies have web sites and you can learn a lot about companies by browsing their web sites. You can generally glean recent news items, company history, and even company culture from a web site. Most web sites have an About Us page that will impart some information about the company. Some web sites will have links to their blogs or newsletters. You can learn a lot about most companies in perusing this information. By the same token, I would also use Google to uncover additional information about the company you'll be interviewing. You should remember that sometimes company websites provide a rosy picture of the company that is contrary to what you might find in searching articles or reviews on Google. Again, I should remind you to be prepared to take this information "with a grain of salt". For example, if you are interested in working for a certain restaurant and you find an article trashing that restaurant on Google, take that article with a grain of salt. It could be an instance in which someone is on a crusade and has an axe to grind against that restaurant. On the other hand, if you see repeated complaints against that restaurant or any other company, you can probably presume that they have a problem in that area.

2) Corporate/Company Culture. If you read between the lines on the company web site or in the company blogs or newsletters, you should be able to get a feel for the corporate culture. If a newsletter describes the company's annual picnic and shows lots of families with

kids, that might mean that it's a company that values its employees and their families. If a company is involved in a lot of outside charitable activities (raising money for the local children's hospital, building and repairing homes as part of Habitat for Humanity, etc.), then you can presume that the company culture includes charitable work in the community. If the newsletters refer to company softball teams, corporate outings, or corporate planning sessions or retreats, you have an additional glimpse into the culture of the company. You can also find out more about a company and its culture by viewing their social media accounts, including platforms such as Facebook, Twitter, Instagram, and LinkedIn.

3) Company History. It's good if you can gather some information about the history of the company. Maybe you'll find out that the company was started by a couple of college buddies in a dorm room or that a company's first fast food restaurant was started in Southern California. Whatever information you find may give you a better indication of where the company came from and how that relates to what it is now. And don't hesitate to "drop" some of the information you learn into your interview conversation whenever appropriate. It won't hurt your chances if the interviewer knows that you took some time to do your homework.

4) The Key Players. In researching a prospective employer, you should determine who the key players are. Whether that is the founder, the owner, the current CEO, or various department heads, it will behoove you to find out what you can about the company's key players. As an example, I have a client of mine who has been on a career track in restaurant marketing for a couple of decades now. When he researches the next company he would like to work for, one of the first things he does is to check to see what the backgrounds of the key players are. Do they all have restaurant backgrounds or do

some of them have non-restaurant backgrounds? Are the key players mostly young or are they older? In reading the bios of one of his recent target companies, my client determined that two of the company bigwigs had the same college alma mater as he did. He also found that a number of them were heavy into golfing as a hobby. My client made a note of this, as he was also an avid golfer. And later on, when the opportunity presented itself, he mentioned his love for golf in an interview and it led to a conversational discussion with the hiring manager, who was also an avid golfer. Bottom line is that my client researched the key players of the company he was interested in working for and he used the information he gained to his advantage, finding common ground with the person who did the interviewing and some of the company's key executives. With the knowledge that his alma mater was the same as a couple of the executives and that one of his favorite pastimes was the same as some of the corporate executives, he was able to establish common ground and give them the indication that he would fit in with the company and its executives.

5) The Interviewer. Hopefully, you can get the name of the person who will be interviewing you and you can then do some quick research on them. If the interviewer is not listed on the company web site, you can certainly check social media platforms and Google to see if you can find a presence. Again, you don't want to go overboard with this, however you might be able to find "common ground" between you and your interviewer with the information you are able to find.

6) Company Competitors. Most companies have competitors and it may be useful for you to find out who those competitors are and how those competitors might affect the company's position.

7) News, Recent Events. Part of this should probably be under the About the Company section, but it's also important enough to have

its own section or mention. You can use the internet to find out all kinds of information about the company you'll be interviewing with. Recent news articles, blogs, or newsletters might tell you about new products they're introducing, new services they're offering, a new branch or location they're opening, their expansion into other countries, etc. As some of this news may relate to the job opening you're applying for, this information might be extremely helpful to you in determining why the company has the opening.

8) Reviews. Just as you search for news and information on the company you'll be interviewing with, you should also check reviews. This can often by simply done in Google by listing the name of the company and then listing the word "reviews" behind it. (i.e.—XYZ reviews). You might be surprised by what you find in reviews. For example, my neighbor's son was looking for a summer job between his first and second year of college. He wanted to work retail and he had a specific retail chain in mind. Before he sent his application to the company he had wanted to target, he searched reviews for this company online. He was surprised to find out that the company he had been interested in was notorious for paying its employees less than many other retail concepts and a number of reviews from ex-employees revealed some reasons why it probably wasn't the great place to work that he thought it might be. So, in his particular situation, researching reviews turned out to be very helpful for this young man and he ended up working for another higher-paying retailer.

9) Inside Scoop. Along the same lines as the abovementioned reviews, you can get additional scoops on prospective employers by searching the internet. Glassdoor.com is a site that can provide inside information regarding many companies. The information provided includes salary figures, employee functions, company reviews, the

hiring process, and other details you can use to your advantage in positioning yourself above other candidates for the same job.

Again, I'd like to emphasize the importance of doing your homework in researching prospective employers. In doing so, you're looking to find information which will place you above the other candidates looking to land the same job. In researching prospective employers, I always remind clients not to ignore seemingly unimportant information. As mentioned above in some of the previous examples, you might be able to use inconsequential information such as college alma maters or love of golf as a pastime to establish common ground with the person you're interviewing with or the company you want to work for. At the worst, you'll at least be able to show your prospective employer that you've taken the time to research their company. At the best, the information you find might be a keystone in helping you show that you're a good fit for the job you're applying for.

Other Vital Ways to Prepare for Your Job Interview.

Here are some additional tips you can use to prepare for your job interview:

Make sure you practice your answers to common interview questions. Most interviews contain the "Tell Me About Yourself" question in some shape or form, so you should definitely have an answer prepared to that question. A commonly asked question which has been the downfall of many job applicants, is the "Describe Your Biggest Weakness" question. This is a difficult question which needs to be handled properly. You probably won't want to say that you don't have any weaknesses, as that may come off as cocky or arrogant. And you won't want to spend a lengthy time describing your weaknesses, as you'll certainly be better served by spending time on your strengths. When my clients ask me how they should handle this question, I tell them to list a specific weakness, but then to also explain how they are working to overcome the weakness. For example, I have a client who is somewhat shy, at least until people get to know him. He's in a public relations position, so his jobs have often entailed speaking in front of groups of people. He's never been comfortable with this, however he's worked to become proficient at it. So, when the interviewer asked him what his biggest weakness is, he replied, "I've never really been comfortable speaking in front of groups. However, I've worked hard at it. I've joined Toastmasters and I've offered myself as a guest speaker or guest presenter at various industry functions. I'm now to the point where I am much more comfortable speaking in front of groups, and I'm still working to get better, but I've improved considerably since I realized that I had some shortcomings as a public speaker. I'm to the point now where I no longer consider it to be a weakness."

Another question you're likely to get in one form or another is, "Why are you interested in this position?" or "Why are you interested in working for our company?" Again, you should have a rehearsed and polished answer to this question. In answering the question, it's important to emphasize what you can do for the company and what you can bring to the table instead of what the company can do for you.

In preparing for an interview, I strongly suggest that you practice answering different questions that might be asked. And practice your answers out loud. It's one thing to have an answer inside your head, but it's another thing to hear how that answer sounds when you express it vocally. I have a client who tells me that he sometimes practices his answers in the shower, instead of singing. Other people will stand in front of mirrors as they practice answering questions. If you have a friend or relative, or even a loyal dog, who will volunteer to be a willing listener as you practice your answers, that will be even better. I've seen the results that mock interviews and practicing answers can produce and I strongly recommend that you include this in your interview preparation arsenal.

Job Interview Preparation

I also encourage people to prepare some questions to answer during the interview. And then, hopefully during the interview, you'll be able to come up with some additional questions to ask of your interviewer. It's OK to jot these questions down on a notepad and bring them with you to the interview. But make sure you stay engaged in the interview and listen to the information the interviewer is providing. You don't want to be asking questions for information the interviewer has already provided.

I also tell people to prepare an interview kit to take to the interview. This includes resumes, a copy of your cover letter, a copy of the job posting, samples of previous work you'd like to show, licenses and certifications, and a vetted reference listed. When I say vetted, I'm strongly suggested that you've already compiled a list of personal and professional references who you've contacted and who have agreed to vouch for you. You'd be surprised how many people list references without even informing them that they've been listed as a reference.

Your interview kit should include at least five or six resumes, as you can never be sure how many people you will meet during the interview process. And don't forget to include things such as paper napkins or tissues, breath mints or breath spray, a stain stick, a lint remover, and even an umbrella. In other words, be prepared.

If you're going to take a bag to your interview, make sure it's cleaned out and you're taking only the essentials you'll need for the interview. If you need someone to help you to carry your bag into the interview room because it's so heavy, you haven't cleaned it out enough. Joke.

And always bring a notebook and pen with you to the interview. That notebook can include any notes or questions you have prepared for the interview, but you can also use it to take notes and write down any questions you have throughout the interview process. Again, it's important that if you're going to take notes during an interview, don't overdo it. You won't want to spend all your time looking down at your notepad when you should be making eye contact and engaging

Job Interview Preparation

with the interviewer. With the notes you bring into any interview, you should be familiar enough with those notes so you don't have to constantly refer to them. And you certainly don't want to read those notes verbatim. I also tell clients to pretend that they are a television newscaster, looking down at their notes occasionally, but spending almost all their time looking at and engaging with the interviewer. And yes, eye contact is extremely important. When you meet someone and when you interview with someone, you need to look them in the eye. When I was a hiring manager, I viewed this as an absolute must. Persons who didn't look me in the eye when I first met with them had already lost points with me.

Body language is important. Stand up straight, sit up straight, and act interested. No slouching or slumping.

Finally, if you're a person for whom conversation or speech doesn't flow smoothly, I suggest that you come up with a go-to phrase that you can use to fill space while you are forming your answers to any interview questions. Some people will simply repeat the question. i.e.—When asked why they're interested in working for the company they're interviewing with, they'll use that question to transition into their answer. "Why am I interested to work for the XYZ Company? Well, among other things, I love the industry and, with my experience and my enthusiasm, I think I could bring a lot to the table." Or, you could respond by saying, "That's a great question. I'd have to say that among the reasons I'd like to work for XYZ Company are the fact that..." You get the picture. If conversation or answering questions doesn't come easy for you, use some go-to phrases to fill the void while you gather your thoughts.

If you want to give yourself the best chance of acing your interview, you should make sure that you prepare for it. In most instances, you'll be competing for jobs against candidates who will certainly do their homework in preparing for the interview. You'll have to make sure that you can match or exceed their efforts if you're going to land the job for which you're interviewing.

Job Interview Preparation

Chapter 4—Questions and Answers

Going into an interview, you can never be sure what kinds of questions you're going to be asked. To help you with this process, I'm going to use my experience as a career counselor and give you both some common questions and some more difficult and challenging questions you might be asked in your interviews. Although I won't be able to give you the exact questions you'll be asked, the questions I've outlined should give you a good idea of what you might be asked in an interview.

12 Common Interview Questions and How to Ace Them.

Along with the common questions you might be asked, I've listed some tips on how you might answer. Although you'll obviously want to provide your own answers, the tips I've provided should give you some ideas on how you might answer the questions.

1)   *"Tell me about yourself."* This is a very commonly asked question, often used near the start of an interview. With this request, the interviewer is trying to get a quick overview of who you are and make sure you're a good fit for the job opening. If you prepare to answer any common interview question, this is the question that you should most definitely practice answering, again and again. It's an important question and since it will almost always appear near the start of any interview, you'll want to immediately try to establish yourself as a formidable candidate; preferably as a candidate who stands above the other candidates. In answering the question, you should provide an overview of your current position and then provide information as to how your current position is relative to the position you're applying for. Also, provide any other highlights from your career or background

Job Interview Preparation

that relate to the job you're applying for. And, it's OK for you to include a few personal details that might help the interviewer to remember you and to separate you from the other candidates. i.e.— "And when I'm not working, I love to spend time with my family. This summer I'm coaching my nine-year-old daughter's softball team. I love it."

2) *"How would you describe yourself?"* When they ask this question, they're not looking for your height, your weight, and your eye color. Provide an answer that coincides with the qualities and abilities they said they're looking for in their job description. If one of the keywords in their job posting referred to someone who can lead a team of employees, you should then make sure that you mention that you are an excellent leader, someone who communicates well, enjoys leading a team, and is good at it. If their job post mentions that they are looking for someone who can take a project from start to finish without a lot of supervision, mention the fact that you can take a project and run with it in your answer. Offer only positive descriptions; try to correlate the description of yourself with the qualities they appear to be looking for in a candidate.

3) *"Why do you want to work here?"* This question offers a chance for you to show that you've done your homework and your research. With your answer, you can point out how the company products, services, history, or culture relates to your interests. For example, when my college student daughter applied for a seasonal position in a bookstore, she was asked this question and she responded in kind: "I love books, I love bookstores, I love telling people about good books, and I love helping people. I've loved coming here as a customer with my parents from the time I was a little girl and I like the way this place makes customers feel like they're valued and welcome. The people who work in this store are always so helpful. I want to be one of those people." In my opinion, this was a terrific answer, as it

Job Interview Preparation

told exactly why she wanted to work there. Admittedly, she was applying for a basic retail position, so she didn't get into a lot of specifics as to what she could bring to the table other than a "can-do" helpful attitude, but she's a college student and doesn't have a lot of work experience. If you're applying for a higher-level position, you can use more tangible and less emotional references on why you want to work there.

4) *"What interests you most about the job you're applying for?"* This question offers you the opportunity to tell how your skills, your experience, or your attitude match up with what they are looking for. Again, I'll remind you that you should think about what you can offer the company with this answer instead of what they can offer you.

5) *"Why are you looking to leave your current job?"* In answering this question, this is not the time to bash your current company or your current position. It's not time to pull out the crying towel or the axe to grind. Don't focus on the negative aspects of your current company or position. Instead, focus on the opportunities or the positives that new job would offer you.

6) *"What are you passionate about?"* Another opportunity to relate your interests and passions to what the prospective employer is looking for. Again, go back to the original job posting and add any other information you've learned about the position you're interviewing for and formulate an answer that shows how your interests and passions fit with what they're looking for in an employee.

7) *"What are your greatest strengths?"* Here's a chance for you to toot your own horn. Again, your answer should relate to the qualities they're looking to find in a new employee. For example, if they are looking for someone who can create and implement new

product introductions, you might respond, "I love developing new product campaigns and I'm good at it. I've done it at my current company and our product rollouts have always been very successful. I can take an introduction from the idea stage to the implementation stage and I can do that without much supervision. I consider myself to be an expert in developing product introductions and I think that's definitely something I can bring to the table in the position you're offering."

8) *"What are your greatest weaknesses?"* We outlined this question in detail earlier in this book, but I will again remind you that this is a bit of a trap question, as you won't want to spend a lot of time focusing on your deficiencies when you'll be better served focusing on your strengths. It probably won't be wise for you to answer that you don't have any weaknesses, as that will likely come across as cocky and arrogant. So, with the answer you give, you will ideally give an example of a legitimate weakness that you have, but then you'll tell the interviewer how you have worked to correct this weakness. Are you a person who can't say "no" and takes on too much? If so, you might note with your answer that you've learned to say "no", you've learned to delegate, or you've learned to ask for help from your team. Are you someone who prefers to do things yourself instead of delegating it to a fellow employee who might not be able to do it as well? If so, explain how you've worked to bridge this weakness. Maybe you've made a more concentrated effort to educate the employee at the start of the project or maybe you meet with the employee a couple times a week throughout the project to make sure that they're progressing as planned. Either way, whatever weakness you unveil to the interviewer, you should make sure you tell them how you've worked to rectify that deficiency.

9) *"What are your goals for the future?/Where do you want to be in five years?"* I'm not a big fan of these questions, but they're often asked nonetheless. In asking either of these questions, a hiring manager is most likely doing one of two things: They're probably trying to find out if you plan to stick around for a while or they want to find out how their company or their position fits into your long-term goals. So, in answering the question, you should again relate how their company and the job they are offering will fit into your plans. If you're interviewing for a restaurant marketing position and tell the interviewer that you want to own a tree trimming company in the next five years, that's probably not going to help you secure the job you're interviewing for. Along the same lines, your answer should never be, "I have no idea." It's doubtful that your prospective employer is going to be interested in hiring an employee who has no idea where he is going with his life.

10) *"Tell me about a difficult work situation you've had and how you handled it?"* With this question, the interviewer is probably trying to determine how you handle adversity and/or to determine if you are able to solve problems. In answering a question like this, you should remember that stories are often more effective than facts and figures. If you have a story you can tell to show how you solved a difficult situation, it will be more memorable that any facts and figures you can relay. i.e.—An events planner has a wedding photographer cancel on her the day of the wedding… A major corporate client announces that he is thinking of taking his business elsewhere because he doesn't feel like he's been getting the proper amount of attention from the salesperson who works for you…You worked in a retail store during the holiday season, the line at the register was about 10 deep, and you had a customer who was loudly complaining about the wait. With any of these situations or your own difficult situation, you should detail how you worked to solve the problem. And, hopefully, it had a happy ending. And, ideally, this problem will relate in some way to the position you're applying for.

11) *"Why should we hire you?"* This is a question that normally appears near the end of the interview. If you get this question, you should consider it a final opportunity for you to reiterate what you can bring to the table and why you'll be a good fit for the job they're offering. Detail again the skills and experience which make you a great candidate to fill the open position. Also, don't be afraid to throw in a more emotional, less tangible statement, such as "I'm sure I'll be a valuable employee", "I assure you that I'll work hard to accomplish the goals you set for me", "I'm very interested in working here and I'm sure I can be a valued member of the team", etc.

12) *"Do you have any questions?"* This question also often appears at or near the end of the interview. It's not a throwaway question and you should never not have any additional questions. This question offers you the opportunity to cover any subjects which were not covered in the interview. Again, you should refer to any questions you had on your notepad before the interview or any questions that may have developed over the course of the interview. If all of your questions have been covered, take the opportunity to turn the remaining interview time into more of a conversation. You could ask the interviewer about their own experiences within the company, ask them what success would look like in the position they are hiring for, or ask them what are some of the challenges you might expect in the role they are hiring for. Either way, don't pass on an opportunity to show the interviewer that you're interested in the job they're offering by asking some pertinent questions. If you don't ask any questions, the interviewer may not think that you're interested in the position.

Navigating Difficult Questions Like a Champion.

Job Interview Preparation

Don't be surprised if you are asked some difficult or challenging questions in your interview. After all, an interview is part of an elimination process and interviewers are looking for ways to separate the competition and determine who the best fit for the job will be.

When I was fresh out of college, I had an interview for a job I really wanted. I prepared diligently for that interview. I practiced answers to lots of different questions by enlisting my friends to conduct mock interviews. Over and over again, I rehearsed the answers to any questions I thought the interviewer might ask. By the time the interview rolled around, I thought that I was ready for just about any question imaginable. About three minutes into the interview, the interviewer asked me a question that left me totally off balance. Her question was, "If you were a tree, what kind of tree would you be and why?" Oops, I hadn't practiced for that one. Why in the world would an interviewer ask a question like that? I didn't have a lot of time to analyze why she asked me that, but I wanted to know what the method to her madness was in asking me that, before I gave my answer. I quickly determined, correctly I think, that she wanted to see if I was able to think outside the box and to see how my thought process was. After stuttering and stammering for just a short time, I replied, "I would be an oak tree. Oak trees are strong and steady and they're useful. Oak trees have a strong root system. When they're in full bloom, they provide shade for others to enjoy. And they provide nuts (acorns) that squirrels, chipmunks, wild turkeys, and other animals can enjoy." By the time I finished answering that question, I was confident that I handled it adequately.

Although there probably wasn't a right or wrong answer to that question, I was happy that I'd been able to provide some decent reasons why I would be an oak tree. I later joked that I was glad that I hadn't said I want to be a weeping willow tree or a sappy maple tree.

A client of mine reports that he was recently asked a similar question in an interview: "If you could be a superhero, what superhero would you be and why?" Again, I'm guessing that the interviewer was trying to determine the applicant's thought process with a question like this. My client, who told me that he really doesn't know of many superheroes, told me that he answered that he would be Batman, as Batman and Superman were the only two superheroes he could think of when he was asked the question. He said that he chose Batman because Batman is/was someone who is very protective. He works well with his associates, including his sidekick Robin and his butler Alfred. He is physically and mentally fit, and intelligent. He has a passion for justice and an interest in protecting people from injustice. My client then added that he was like Batman in that he works well with his co-workers, he tries to stay physically and mentally fit, and, as a loyal employee, he always wants to make things right if they're wrong.

Not a bad answer from my friend, I think. He showed that he could think through the answer to a challenging question and then draw it all back into how Batman's qualities and his own qualities would make him a viable fit for the job he was applying for.

In the previous section on common interview questions, I've already listed some common questions which I'd consider to be challenging questions. Questions like "Where do you want to be in five years?", "Can you tell me about a difficult situation you've previously had in a job and how you handled it?", and "What are your weaknesses?" are all commonly asked and challenging interview questions. How you answer those questions may well determine whether you move ahead in the interview process. With this in mind, I strongly suggest that you practice your answers to these questions.

For the fun of it, I've gathered a few other challenging questions for you to consider when you do your mock interviews. Although the chances that you'll be asked these specific questions are very minimal, you should use these questions to hone your thought process in formulating rational and reasonable answers to difficult questions.

Job Interview Preparation

Although I won't list answers for these questions, as many of them are thought process questions that don't have specific right or wrong answers, I'm hoping that these questions will provide some food for thought as you prepare for your interview.

Here goes:

1) *"If you were a car, what kind of car would you be and why?"*

2) *"Why do you think you'd be successful at the job you're applying for?"*

3) *"Can you explain the employment gap in your resume?"*

4) *"What can you offer us as an employee that other candidates can't?"*

5) *"If you could host a dinner people with four famous people, dead or alive, who would you invite and why?"*

6) *"How do you manage and prioritize your time?"*

7) *"Can you tell me about a time in the past where you were innovative or 'thought outside the box'?"*

8) *"How to you deal with conflict?"*

9) *"Can you describe an ethical dilemma that you've previously faced and how you handled it?"*

Job Interview Preparation

10)   "What has been the biggest failure in your life?"

11)   "How did you make time for this interview? Where does your boss think you are now?"

12)   " Have you ever stolen office supplies from a company you've worked for?"

13)   "Can you tell me about a company policy you're disagreed with and whether and how you expressed you displeasure with that policy?"

14)   "Can you tell me a reason why people might not like working with you?"

15)   "What would you do if you won $10 million in this week's lottery?"

And there's one more question I'd like to discuss briefly in this chapter. You may be asked this question or something similar: "What salary do you think you deserve?" This is obviously a key question for both the prospective employer and for the candidate, as if the amount offered by the employer is too low or the amount tendered by the applicant is too high, it can easily be a dealbreaker. As an interview candidate, you will have hopefully researched what salaries are in the job category you're interested in. If you haven't researched, you'll find plenty of available salary information on the internet, including sites like indeed.com, glassdoor.com, payscale.com, and LinkedIn.com. In reviewing the salary ranges for your profession, you should always keep in mind the cost of living in the city where you'll be working. Obviously, the cost of living in New York City or San

Francisco will be much higher than it will be for a similar job in Dyersville, Iowa.

When you are asked this salary question, I would highly recommend that you don't give a specific salary. You should first ask the interviewer to confirm the salary range for the job they're offering. For example, if they tell you that the job they are offering is in the $40,000 to $50,000 annual salary range, you'll then at least have a starting point for your negotiations. In most instances, I'd recommend that you request a salary which is higher than the median, unless there's a logical reason why you might be given less than the median. (i.e.—You're less experienced than the other candidates, you're a recent college grad and the other candidates have had previous industry experience, etc.)

Ideally, you won't talk salary on the first interview unless the interviewer is ready to hire you on the spot. If you're applying for a retail position in a department store, you'll probably be discussing salary during the initial interview. If you're applying for an executive position, it's more likely for salary to be discussed in a later interview. In this instance, I would avoid talking salary and compensation package in the initial interview unless the interviewer broaches the subject first.

In reading this section of the book, if there's one thing you can take away from what you've read, I'm hoping that you now understand that the key to answering interview questions, common or challenging, is to prepare and practice. Although the questions you practice answering are likely not to be the same questions you get in the actual interview, it's important that you practice the thought processes you'll need to answer questions you're not familiar with. With preparation and practice, you'll be sure to increase your chance of acing the interview.

Chapter 5—Make a Great First Impression

The first impression you make as you head into your interview can be crucial. I always tell clients that even though it's unlikely that they'll get a job based on their first impression, it's more likely possible that they could lose a job based on their first impression. People who make bad first impressions can lose chances at jobs even before they get a chance to explain what their background, their talents and skills, and why they are the right fit for the job.

With this in mind, I've provided some simple tips on things you can do to make sure you make a great first impression.

Eight Things You Must Do to Make a Killer First Impression.

1) Dress the Part. In an earlier section, I explained the importance of dressing properly for your interview. Again, the main thing you should concentrate on is to make sure that you are properly dressed for the job you're applying for. If you're not exactly sure what to wear, you should remember that it's better to dress up for an interview than it is to dress down.

2) Show Up on Time. As mentioned before, you're certainly going to lose points if you show up late for an interview. We've discussed this previously. If you're going to be late, maybe because of unusually heavy traffic or unusually bad driving conditions, you should certainly call the person you're interviewing with as soon as you realize that you're going to be late. It's not a good idea to keep someone waiting; it's worse to keep someone waiting when they don't know you're going to be late. On the other hand, I've not mentioned before that you should try not to arrive too early for an interview. You should not arrive any earlier than 30 minutes ahead of an interview. If

you do arrive much earlier than expected, the interviewer may feel rushed or uncomfortable in trying to accommodate you.

3) Be Nice to Everyone. When you're interviewing for a job, it's important that you "put your game face on" as soon as you enter the premises. Be nice to everyone you meet by greeting them with a smile and/or a hello. This includes people you meet in the parking lot, people you meet in the elevator, people you pass in the hall, and certainly the receptionist. Two quick stories: One of my clients was primping on an elevator as she rode up to the third floor for her interview. She looked at herself in her compact mirror, made sure her teeth didn't contain any food particles, made sure her hair looked good. As she did this, she basically ignored the only person who rode up in the elevator with her. You guessed it, the person who rode up in the elevator with her was the person who she was interviewing with. When my client discovered this, she was frantic in trying to remember what she had done in front of the person she rode the elevator with and she was embarrassed to think that she hadn't at least greeted the other person riding in the elevator. Another of my clients carried on a conversation with the receptionist in the lobby at the company where he was interviewing. The receptionist wasn't very busy. It seems that her primary responsibility was to answer the phones and the phones weren't ringing, so the receptionist was open to a chat. After my client was hired, he found out that the interviewer's best friend was the receptionist and the interviewer routinely solicited the receptionist's first impression of the people who interviewed there. Thanks to his pleasant conversation with the receptionist, my client got some bonus points even before his official interview began. So, bottom line is, when you go to an interview, it's important for you to get into the mindset of being friendly to everyone you meet. You never know when the impressions you make will impact your chances of getting a job.

4) Put Your Phone Away. It's obvious that you'll want to turn your phone off during the interview itself. But I suggest that you put it away from the time you enter the lobby. I'll note below the importance of being engaged during an interview. You can't be engaged in an interview if you're spending time on your phone. Back in the days in which I was interviewing for jobs, I always found the time I spent in the lobby waiting for the interview to be educational. It was interesting to see how the receptionist greeted other visitors and co-workers. It was also interesting to see how the company's workers interacted with each other. In one of my interviews, in the 20 minutes I spent in the lobby, I noticed that the body language and the interactions of the people who worked at that company were unusually negative. As a result, even before I went into the interview, I was questioning whether I wanted to work there. Sure enough, the human resources person was out of the same negative mold and I left the building knowing that I would not accept the offer I received. I was glad that I had put my phone away and was cognizant of what the workplace environment was.

5) Be Engaged, Be Interested. In interviewing for any job, it's important that you show your interest or enthusiasm. I always tell clients to make sure they are engaged from the time they enter the door of the office or the door of the building in which they are interviewing. Pay attention to the things that are visible in the lobby and in the office of the person you're interviewing with. An average interview might last 45 minutes. Those 45 minutes could be a major factor in determining your future. With this in mind, any interview you have deserves your undivided attention and your undeterred enthusiasm.

6) Be Confident. It's important that you look confident going into an interview. Pay attention to your body language, your posture, and your demeanor. When you meet someone, make sure to introduce yourself, offer a firm handshake, and make eye contact. I've noted

before that whenever I've been the interviewer, I've docked applicants who have a flimsy handshake or failed to look me in the eye when they're introduced to me.

7) Make Sure You Know Who You're Talking To. This seems so obvious, but I've had clients who've made the grave error of calling their interviewer by the wrong name throughout the interview. I had a client who addressed Janel as Jolene throughout the interview and I'm sure she lost some serious points for doing so. Make sure you have the interviewer's name going into the interview. It's desirable to use the name of the interviewer(s) throughout the interview, but you have to make sure you're using the right name.

8) Find Common Ground, Make a Connection. With any interview, it's important for you to make a connection or find common ground with the people you're interviewing with. Again, you'll probably be competing against other candidates in getting the job, and you'll want to separate yourself from those other candidates by possibly making a connection with the person who was interviewing you. From the time you enter the building, or the conference room or office where the interview is being conducted, you should observe your surroundings to see if you can find anything that will help you to make a connection with the interviewer. Are there company newsletters in the lobby for guests to read, a company trophy case or history case? What personal belongings do you spot in the office of your interviewer? Family photos, softball or bowling trophies, college diploma, etc. Can you use any of these things to find common ground? Many years ago, I was trying to get the business of a man who would later become a big client for my company. Upon meeting him for the first time in his office, I noted that he had a baseball trophy on one of the shelves in his office and also he had a framed version of a Minnesota Twins baseball pennant and World Series tickets hanging on his wall. I surmised immediately that this man was a baseball fan

and, as an avid baseball fan myself, I started our conversation off by asking him if he was a baseball fan. Sure enough, he was, and we found common ground immediately. To this day, I swear that one of the reasons I was able to secure his business was because we had a common love of baseball. Of course, none of this would have mattered if my company hadn't been a good fit for his business, but our mutual love of baseball allowed me to separate myself from other candidates immediately. I've had clients that have been able to do the same thing with mutual alma maters, comparing kids ("Are these your sons? I have three sons…."),etc. If you can find common ground or make a connection with your interviewer, you're likely to enhance your chances of landing the job.

How to Instantly Stand Out Among Other Candidates.

As I've noted before, job interviews are a competition of sorts. There are multiple candidates for almost all job openings and if you're going to get the job you're probably going to have to stand out from your competition. If you don't, you're likely to be forgotten quickly.

When my clients ask me how they can stand out in an interview, I have a number of suggestions on how to do so:

I've previously noted how important it is for you to do your homework heading into an interview. One of the surest ways to stand out in an interview is to know more about the company than anyone else. Most interviews offer plenty of opportunities to show that they've done their research and to show how much they know about the company. Obviously, the questions you ask during an interview can also show that you've researched the company thoroughly. If you don't show the interviewer that you know anything about the company you're interviewing with, they're likely to think that you're not very interested in the job.

Another way to stand out in an interview is to simply be yourself. I encourage clients to be themselves during an interview, if only because so many people are not good at pretending to be someone we are not. We're not play actors and if you're trying to be someone else during the interview, most interviewers will be able to detect that. Another reason I encourage clients to be themselves is because if they actually land the job, the employer is probably going to find out quickly who the employee really is anyway. So, as strange as it sounds, you can stand out in an interview by being yourself.

And here's an important way for you to stand out. Treat your interviews like conversations. Interviewing is a two-way street. You're not going to make a good impression if you treat the interview like a college exam or a police interrogation, with the interviewer asking all the questions and you dutifully providing all the answers. It's important that you try to turn the interview into a conversation. You can do this by asking related questions throughout the interview process. Again, as I've mentioned many times before, if you're going to turn the interview into a conversation instead of an interrogation, you're going to have to be totally engaged in what's being said throughout the interview. Listen intently and then ask questions or add comments as you see fit. A good way to do this is to end your answer with a related question. For example, if you're asked why you think you're a good fit for the job you're interviewing for, you might say, "From everything I've read or heard about this company, it is a company that cares deeply about its customers. I'm the same way. I derive a great deal of satisfaction in knowing that my customers value the products and services I sell. This company seems to do a better job of that than its competitors. Am I right in thinking that and can you share why you think that is?" Note that the interviewee has answered the question and then followed it up with a related question of their own, a question which is not a yes or no question, one that will hopefully help turn the interview into more of a conversation than an interrogation or exam.

Job Interview Preparation

Another way to stand out in an interview will be to provide an additional one-sheet summary, other than your resume and your cover letter, explaining why you're a good fit for the specific job you're applying for. I've had some clients who will present this summary during the interview and other clients who will send this summary after an interview. Some of my clients swear by this technique, regardless of whether it's presented during or after the interview. I've also had clients who have submitted 30-, 60-, or 90-day plans on what they would hope to accomplish in their first days of working for the company. These plans are almost always presented in the days immediately following the interview (obviously before the company has made a hiring decision). In doing something additional to just the standard resume and cover letter, you'll be able to reiterate your sincere interest in the job.

If the interviewer asks you for examples of how you've been successful in your previous jobs, I'll remind you again to use numbers whenever possible to document your success. i.e.—"I was responsible for increasing sales in the Northeast Region by 135% in the first two years I had that region." Or another example: "As a franchise development director, we went from 45 franchised print shops to 87 franchised print shops within a year. The company goal when I arrived there was to open 20 locations per year and my team and I were able to exceed that by 22 locations." Bottom line is that numbers work in illustrating success and achievement. With numbers, you can turn an intangible statement into a tangible one.

And, finally, another way for you to stand out after an interview is the send a handwritten thank you/enjoyed meeting you note. Yes, I said handwritten, not typed. Handwritten is so much more personal than a typed note. If the company is very close to you, you might even hand-deliver it. If not, you can send it via the US Post Office or a delivery service, but send it immediately, within 24 hours. And, obviously make sure your spelling, grammar, and punctuation are correct.

Confident Body Language that Puts You Ahead of the Game.

So, you think you've done everything possible to make a great first impression. You're impeccably dressed, you polished your shoes, got a haircut, and manicured your nails. Yet, if you don't pay attention to the signals your body is sending, your body can work against you and impair the image you're trying to convey with your appearance. Body language is important. We all know people who can capture a room when they walk into it. In just a matter of seconds, people will form perceptions on a person based on their body language. So, all the time and money you spent for the new suit, the haircut, and even the new leather portfolio can all get blown to bits in just a moment.

One of the key elements of body language is proper posture. If you want to display an air of confidence, it's important that you "walk tall"…stand straight, chin up, eyes up. Certainly, no slumping or slouching. Nothing worse than slinking into a room.

I've already mentioned the importance of a firm handshake when being introduced to someone. Yes, there's an art to doing something as simple as a handshake. When you're introduced to your interviewer, put away your floppy fish handshake and replace it with your "big boy" handshake. Male or female, you should offer a firm, genuine handshake. That being said, don't shake hands so firmly that you're going to crush the other person's hand. Always stand, and never sit, when you are shaking hands. Don't pull the other person toward you with your handshake…it's not an arm wrestling match. And avoid sweaty hands. And beware that there are some people who do not want to shake hands. Most of us know some people who are germophobes who try to avoid physical contact whenever possible. If you run into an interviewer who is a germophobe, don't take it personally.

Job Interview Preparation

At the same time you're shaking hands with someone, you need to make eye contact with them. And continue to do that as much as possible throughout the interview. In making eye contact with someone, you'll exude a sense of confidence, genuineness, and sincerity. Remember that one of your goals for the interview will be to create a bond or a connection with your interviewer. Eye contact can help you do that. If you're looking down at the floor or over at the wall when you're shaking hands with your interviewer, you may well give them the idea that you're insecure.

Besides your posture and your eyes, pay attention to what you're doing with your arms and legs throughout the interview. Don't cross your legs, when you're standing or sitting. Don't place your hands on your hips when you're standing. Don't lean toward one side. Don't cross your arms over your chest at any time. Body language experts will tell you that's a defensive position that doesn't play well with the person you're meeting with.

And pay attention to what you're doing with your hands throughout the interview. If you're someone who does a lot of hand gesturing, don't do any pointing, as that can come across as threatening. Open palm/open hand gestures are considered OK. If you are a bit of a fidgeter, try not to tap your fingers or your toes during the interview.

And don't play with your hair, repeatedly click your pen, jiggle the coins in your pockets, etc. Some of those quirks or bad habits are likely to make a bad impression with the people you meet in your interview.

And finally, smile whenever it is appropriate. And don't be afraid to show those pearly whites, unless you have bad teeth. I can speak from personal experience in regards to facial expressions. People have told me before that I have a stern face. Since that look tends to make me look grumpy or unapproachable, whenever I meet someone in person now, I make sure to make an extra effort to offer a big smile that will make me more welcoming and more approachable.

So, in recapping this chapter, let me again emphasize the importance of making a good first impression in an interview. Although you probably won't be able to land the job with the good first impression you make, you could lose a chance at a job with a bad first impression. That's why you should not ignore the visual impression you are making with the interview. By paying attention to a few minor details, you'll be assured that you've not lost the job before the interview actually starts.

Chapter 6—Pass with Flying Colors

As you interview for jobs, you'll have an advantage toward getting the job of your dreams if you have an understanding of what interviewers want to hear. Along the same lines, you'll benefit from knowing some things you should never say in an interview. And then, you'll also want to convey to the interviewer that you have the soft skills which will ensure your standing as a valuable employee and place you above the other candidates for the same job. (For those of you who aren't familiar with soft skills, I'll explain that in more detail later in this chapter.)

11 Things Your Prospective Employer Wants to Hear.

When you interview for a job, you'll likely be asked a lot of questions. Some job candidates make the mistake of not understanding why the interviewer is asking the questions they're asking. If you have a feel for why your interviewer is asking the questions they're asking, you'll find it much easier to determine the things they want to hear from you. Here are some things that interviewers love to hear from candidates, in no particular order.

1)   *"I'm self-motivated. If you give me a project, I can take it from start to finish...and I can get it done in time. You won't have to micromanage me. I can work with minimal supervision."*

2)   *"I take direction well. You won't have to tell me the same thing multiple times. If you tell me what to do once, you won't have to tell me again."*

3) *"I am a good communicator. I'll keep you and my co-workers updated on any projects I'm working on."*

4) *"I work and play well with others. I'm a team player, not a lone wolf."*

5) *"I can lead or I can follow. I do both well."*

6) *"I'm teachable. I'm quick to admit that I don't know everything and I'm willing and anxious to learn from others."*

7) *"I have the skills to do the job."* (Reiterate your skills here.)

8) *"I'm a good fit for this job and I'm a good fit for this company."* (Detail why you're a good fit here.)

9) *"I'm loyal. I'll be loyal to my supervisor and loyal to the company."*

10) *"My goals and objectives coincide with the mission and purpose of this company."*

11) *"I want to say again that I would love the opportunity to work here."* (Presuming that you're still excited about the job as the interview nears its conclusion, you should reiterate your interest and enthusiasm toward the job before you leave the interview. If you want the job, you should make sure they know that you want the job.)

Eight Things You Won't Want to Say in a Job Interview.

Job Interview Preparation

Just as there are some things you should definitely try to mention in your interview, there are things that you should not say in an interview. I've listed some common mistakes people make in interviews below. Hopefully, these mistakes will give you an idea of what not to say during an interview.

1) *"So, what do you do here?"* Someone hasn't done their homework.

2) *"I know I don't have much experience, but..."* No need to point out your shortcomings and to display a lack of confidence at the same time. If the interviewer has your resume or application, they'll already know that you are short on experience.

3) *"I didn't get along with my boss"* or *"I didn't like the last company I worked for."* Trashing past employers is not going to be helpful.

4) *"How much vacation time do I get?"* This is better discussed in a subsequent interview when you are discussing salary or the compensation package.

5) *"I'd like to start my own business as soon as possible."* Why should someone hire you when you're looking to leave as soon as possible.

6) *"I'll do whatever you want me to do."* Sounds way too desperate.

7) *"How soon do you promote employees."* Again, this comes across as desperate and will probably make the interviewer think that you can't wait to get past the position they're hiring for.

8) *"No, I don't have any questions."* I've discussed this previously. If the interviewer asks if you have any questions, don't pass up the opportunity to ask relevant questions. Not only can you use the questions to gain any additional information you're looking for, you'll be able to convey your interest in the position to the interviewer.

10 Soft Skills and How to Demonstrate Them.

When we talk about demonstrating soft skills, I realize that some of you may not know what soft skills are. With this in mind, let me first tell you what soft skills are. Soft skills are personal attributes, personality traits, social cues, or communication abilities. Soft skills are generally a lot less tangible qualities than hard skills. Hard skills are specific job skills or certifications. Examples of hard skills are high school diplomas, college or trade school degrees, professional licenses or certifications, training program completions, on-the-job training, job experience, etc. Hard skills are specific and tangible job skills or proof of job skills. Soft skills are less tangible qualities that are normally not graded by degrees, certificates, or licenses.

When a company is evaluating your resume, they'll generally look first at the hard skills you've listed on your resume. They want to make sure that your hard skills comply with their requirements and also they'll probably want to compare your hard skills with those of the other candidates. For example, if they're looking for an accounting manager, they're generally going to be looking for someone who has an accounting degree and possibly someone who has passed the CPA

Board Exam. Those are tangible, hard skills. If you don't have those hard skills, you're likely to be eliminated from the competition.

After these prospective employers have determined your hard skills, they'll then move to your soft skills. If you've "passed" the hard skill requirements, it's likely that whether or not you get the job will be determined by your soft skills. Below I've listed some of the most common soft skills that employers are looking for. As you know, most resumes and cover letters have limited space. Although I encourage you to incorporate your soft skills into your resumes and cover letters, I am aware that there's rarely enough room for you to list all of your soft skills. As a result, it's very important that you mention that you have these skills in your interview. In listing soft skills on your resume, I suggest that you label them as "Transferable Skills", as those are qualities that can usually be transferred to just about any job you're applying for.

For the most part, soft skills are acquired over a period of time instead of in classes or training sessions. Whereas someone can get a journalism major by taking college journalism classes, people generally don't get soft skills such as communication skills, creative skills, or problem-solving skills by taking classes. These soft skills are normally acquired by "learning through experience", or the "school of hard knocks" as some would say.

Soft skills are often considered invaluable by employers, as they are transferable skills that can be used in just about any job. Customer service jobs or jobs in which employees come into direct contact with customers are particularly conducive to soft skills.

In determining which soft skills you want to promote, you should read the posting for that position and you note any soft skills which are mentioned in that posting. These are skills that you should be sure to work into your resume, your cover letter, and your interview, presuming you have the skills they are describing.

Job Interview Preparation

For example, if the job posting mentions that the company is looking for someone to become part of their team or the key words in the posting include words such as "team", "teamwork", or "works with others", you'll then know that the company is looking for someone who has this skill. Almost all job postings mention at least a couple of soft skills that the employer is looking for.

Here are some common soft skills which companies are looking for in the people they hire:

1) Motivated or self-motivated.
2) Hard worker or strong work ethic.
3) Adaptability.
4) Team player, able to work well with others.

5) Communicator.
6) Creative thinker, think outside the box, critical thinking.
7) Decision making.
8) Able to resolve conflicts or solve problems.
9) Time management, ability to prioritize.
10) Positivity, enthusiasm.

Again, prior to your interview, you should review the soft skills which are mentioned in the job posting and take an inventory of your own soft skills to see which skills correspond to those that the prospective employer is looking for. Then, you should develop a plan on how you can let the interviewer know you have these skills. For example, if the posting mentions that the employer is looking for a hard worker and you are indeed a hard worker, you'll need to figure out how to drop this into your interview. It won't matter whether you drop this information into the interview directly or indirectly, but you definitely need to let the interview know that you are a hard worker.

Job Interview Preparation

If you can provide specific examples to show that you are a hard worker, that's even better. For example, a client of mine was interviewing for a public relations job in which the primary responsibility included events planning. The posting for this job had mentioned that the company was looking to hire someone that was willing to work hard if necessary to complete a project. So, during her interview, my client mentioned that she was a hard worker and she was willing to work whatever hours were necessary to meet the goals of the department or to complete projects on time. She gave the specific example of how she had coordinated a milk carton boat race in one of her previous jobs. (Yes, boats made of milk cartons.) Her company had been the sole sponsor of this event and her supervisor and the management team had underestimated the amount of time it would take to put this even together. As a result, my client and her two team members had to work 12-hour days, 7 days a week in the two weeks prior to the event to make sure that it went off as planned. As a result of the work of her and her team members, the event went off flawlessly and she received plenty of thank you's from company executives who recognized her hard work and a special thank you from the supervisor who had underestimated the amount of time it would take to plan the event.

As you can see, my client not only mentioned that she was a hard worker, she also told a story that showed that she was a hard worker, willing to do whatever was necessary to make the event a success.

I'll give you another example. Another company looking for a customer service representative mentioned that they were looking for candidates who were problem solvers. One of my clients was applying for this job with a promotional products company, a company that provides custom-imprinted items such as t-shirts, pens, tote bags, etc. for corporate customers. My client had previous experience with a promotional products company and he told this story when asked to describe a problem situation in a previous job and how she handled it. A customer had ordered daily calendar refills every year for many years. One year, the customer was delayed in placing their order and by the time my client went to order these calendar refills for her customer, the factory was sold out of them and they were not going to be getting more of these refills, as they were made in Malaysia and the delivery time to receive additional refill pads was going to be well into March or April of the upcoming year. Instead of just dropping this problem back into her customer's lap, my client worked immediately to find another factory that had similar, but not identical, refills that would work. She had to do about three hours of research and make about a dozen phone calls to come up with a solution to the problem, but she did. She then contacted her customer to make them aware of the initial problem and, at the same time, explain that she had found a solution. She immediately offered to send the customer a photo of the alternate calendar refill pads and the customer found them to be acceptable. All of this for a customer who was placing a small order of about $150.

This story certainly showed my client's ability to attack a problem and solve it, despite the small size of the order. It shows that she was able to go "above and beyond" to solve a problem on behalf of her customer.

If you can find a way to effectively communicate your soft skills to your interviewer, you'll give yourself a much better chance to land the job.

Job Interview Preparation

Chapter 7—Finishing Touches

With this chapter, I'm going to tell you how to put the finishing touches on what will hopefully be a successful interview. I'll give you some questions you can ask the interviewer, I'll tell you how to broach the salary and compensation package discussion, and I'll tell you what to do when and if a question catches you off-guard. And we'll also discuss if and when it's OK to lie or embellish during an interview.

11 Great Questions to Ask the Hiring Manager.

As we've discussed before, the more you can turn your interview into a conversation instead of an interrogation or an exam, the more successful you'll be. Remember, interviews are two-way streets. The interviewer should not be the only person gathering information. You should also be asking the questions you'll need to know about the job you're applying for.

Toward the end of almost every interview, the interviewer or hiring manager is likely to ask you if you have any questions. As we've discussed before, the worst possible way to answer this question is to say that you don't have any questions. If you do this, the interviewer is likely to think that you're either unprepared or you're disinterested.

You should view this question from the interviewer as an opportunity to gather any additional information you're looking for and also to emphasize again the qualities, skills, experience, and reason why you're a good fit for the job.

Again, I strongly suggest that you prepare some questions in advance, at least a half-dozen. And then, as the interview winds down and you get asked if you have any questions, you should select two or three questions to ask of the interviewer. As the interviewer is likely to answer some of the questions you had prior to the interview, make sure you don't ask questions requesting information for subjects that have already been covered. If you do that, the interviewer will know for sure that you weren't paying attention to what he or she said during the interview. On the other hand, as you and the interviewer talk during the interview, you're likely to come up with some additional questions that are more pertinent than the questions you had originally intended to ask.

Below are some of the types of questions you might ask of the interviewer during this part of the conversation. A few quick things before we get into these sample questions: When you ask questions of the interviewer, try not to ask them questions that have yes or no answers. Ask them questions that they can expound upon. And, on the other hand, don't ask questions which are going to stump them or which they're not going to know the answers to. For example, if you're interviewing with the human resources person for an advertising position, you shouldn't be asking them technical questions about advertising methods or advertising philosophies. Those questions will be better asked of the ad director who you are likely to meet in a subsequent interview. And finally, although I'll cover this in more detail later, the first question out of your mouth should not be "What's the salary?" In my previous experiences as an interviewer, I had an applicant ask me this question less than two minutes into the interview. I immediately ruled him out as a candidate and cut what was supposed to be a 45-minute interview to a 20-minute interview. I also had another candidate ask, soon after he sat down, "So, what do you all do here?". I immediately knew that he hadn't done any research, other than maybe how to drive to the interview, and I ruled him out immediately.

Here are some questions you might ask in your interviewer when you get the opportunity to do so:

Job Interview Preparation

1) *"Can you tell me a bit about the company culture or what's it's like to work here?"* This is something you'll definitely want to find out before you accept the position.

2) *"What are the next steps in the interview process?". "When are you looking to have someone on board for this position?"* And if you're meeting with a human resources person or a hiring manager, you should definitely find out who you'll be reporting to and if you'll be able to meet that person during the interview process.

3) *"Will this job offer an eventual opportunity for advancement?" "Can you tell me if any of the people who previously held this position advanced in the company or in their career path?"*

4) *"Is this a new position or are you looking to fill a position that someone previously filled? And, if you don't mind me asking, what did the person who previously filled this position go on to do?"* Or, you can simply ask, *"Why is this job open or available?"*

5) *"Does this job require a lot of travel?" "Is there any chance that I'd be relocated in this position?"*

6) *"What are the company's plans for growth and development? "What are the department's plans?"*

7) *"What's the best part of working for this company?" "What's the most challenging part?"* Again, another question that might help you gain some additional insight regarding the company culture.

8) *"Is there anything I can clarify for you regarding my qualifications?"* This question might help you identify if the

interviewer has any concerns and, if so, you'll then be able to address those concerns.

9) In the unlikely scenario that the interviewer hasn't explained the responsibilities of the job, you should ask. Along the same lines, you might ask, *"Can you give me an idea of what a typical day in this position might look like?"*

10) *"What's an average work week look like? Do most employees put in a lot of extra hours?"*

11) And finally, *"What's next?"* or *"When might I expect to hear from you?"*, *"When would you like me to contact you?"* or *"Is it OK if I follow up in a couple of days?"* Don't leave the interview without finding out what the next step is. If you leave without getting this information, you'll have to spend a lot of time guessing whether you're still in the running for the job or not.

An Essential Guide to Salary Negotiations.

Depending on the job you apply for, you may have the opportunity to negotiate salary. Of course, there are some jobs in which the salary level is already set. My neighbor's son recently interviewed for a job as a seasonal salesperson in a retail chain. It's obvious that a position in a structured corporate environment like this is going to have pre-determined salary structures and you're not going to be able to negotiate your salary as an entry level employee. These are jobs that are what I call single interview jobs, in which only one interview is required before an applicant will be extended an offer or eliminated from the competition.

Job Interview Preparation

On the other hand, most multiple interview situations allow for some salary negotiations. Now, while we can all claim that money should never be the main factor in which to take a job, you also have to remember that the amount you're paid may well have an effect on how you perceive the job. If you're not happy with the salary you're getting or you feel that your salary doesn't properly reflect the talents and abilities you bring to the company, you may find that your salary (or lack of it) makes you discouraged, resentful, or even angry. If you're disappointed in the salary you're making, you may even find that your disappointment leads to poor performance.

In my previous work life, I worked for a company that was notorious for underpaying its employees. It was a great place to work…except for the salaries they paid their employees. As a result of this reputation, employees who worked for this company were the frequent targets of headhunters or corporate recruiters who were looking to place people in different jobs. At that time, I was a rising young executive inside the company and I held a position that carried a lot of responsibility. I was a hard worker and very good at what I did; even my supervisors said so. In this position, I frequently received calls from headhunters offering me interviews for similar positions that paid much higher salaries. As a 26-year-old, I wasn't looking to leave a company I liked working for, but I was fully aware that a higher salary might help me get out of the position of living check-to-check. I was hoping to pay off my college loans and then purchase a modest house. Some of the interview opportunities the headhunters described included salaries that were more than double what I was making and, generally, those jobs carried a lot less responsibility than the job I had. So, it was deflating to know that I wasn't paid fairly. I resisted the weekly requests for interviews for quite a while, but eventually my salary level tainted my perception of the job I had. I eventually started to accept some of the interview invitations and eventually accepted a job that offered almost three times what I had been making.

The moral of the story is that regardless of how unimportant salary might seem, you'll still have bills to pay and you'll still want to make sure you're paid fairly. If you're not paid fairly, you'll probably find that your lack of salary will likely impact your attitude and possibly affect your performance.

Hopefully, you'll have an idea going into the interview what the "market rates" are for the job you're interested in. If you're not sure, you can use various internet sites to obtain salary information. Sites such as indeed.com, glassdoor.com, and LinkedIn all offer industry salary information that you can use as a guideline.

It's important to note that salary is generally discussed near the end of an interview situation. In a multiple interview situation, you might first have a phone interview and/or a video interview before you actually interview with someone face to face. In these instances, you'll find that salary is rarely discussed in the initial interviews. That being said, you should never wait until the very end of an interview to discuss salary or the compensation package. Salary should not be an afterthought and, if you wait too long to discuss salary, you'll lose some of the leverage you might have in negotiating it.

Normally the interviewer will be first to broach the topic, but if they are not doing that and it seems like it's time to discuss salary, you can segue into this discussion by asking something like, "Would now be a good time to talk salary?"

Ideally, you'll be able to get the interviewer to give you a salary range before you have to give up too much information regarding your salary requirements. Some interviewers are likely to ask you what your salary is in your current position. If you're asked this question, I encourage you to be careful not to impart too much information. If you blurt out your current salary, you'll almost certainly be restricting the salary you would be offered in the new job. For example, if you're making an annual salary of $40,000 and you tell the interviewer that, you're likely not to get a salary that exceeds your existing salary by more than 10%. Research shows that many employers are reluctant to increase salaries of new employees substantially if they know the new employee's current salary level and they feel that an increase of around 10% is enough to get someone to leave another job.

So, ideally, you will ask the prospective employer if they have a salary range in mind for the job. If they continue to press you for your current salary, you might respond by saying, "What I make in my current position really isn't relevant, as this would be a different job with a different company and different responsibilities. I'm just looking for a job that will pay me fairly based on my talents and abilities." And then you might add the question, "Can you tell me what kind of budget range you have for this position?"

It should be noted that I would never recommend that you lie about your current salary. Although some people do that, and do it successfully, you should know that if you get caught in a lie, you'll blow your chance to get the job immediately. Also remember that you might have filled out an application on which you were asked to list your current salary. In filling out this portion of an application, I tell my clients to list their desired salary on this line of the application. I.e.—(Desired salary range is $50,000/year.)

So, again, try not to volunteer your current salary information too quickly (unless you're already paid about market rate. In disclosing your salary, you're likely to lose some of your leverage in negotiating a higher salary.

What to Do When You Get a Question that Throws You Off-Guard.

Regardless of how long or how hard you prepare for an interview, you're likely to get one or two questions that will throw you off-guard. Don't let these questions fluster you or "throw you for a loop". I have

Job Interview Preparation

some simple tips which will allow you more time to gather your thoughts.

You can buy more time to develop your answer by simply acknowledging the question. Here are some sample acknowledgments:

>   *--"Oh, that's a good question."*

>   *--"Oh, I've never been asked that before."*

>   *--"Let me think about that for a moment."*

>   *--If you think you can come up with a good answer to the question, you might say, "I'm glad you asked that."*

Another way to buy more time is to simply rephrase or repeat the question. "If I were a tree, what kind of tree would I be and why?" or "So, what kind of tree would I be?"

And, if you don't totally understand the question, you can ask the interviewer to clarify the question. "I want to make sure I understand the question. Can I ask you to expand on that or to clarify?"

And, finally, if the question asked of you is a multi-layered question, feel free to jot down some notes as to how you might answer. But if you're taking notes, make sure that you take them quickly. You won't want to hold up the interview while you take notes.

Is It OK to Lie?; When Is It OK to Lie in an Interview?

Job Interview Preparation

It's no secret that some people lie in interviews. Maybe it's the pressure of getting that job that you really want. Maybe it's the idea, sometimes true, that lying, embellishing, or omitting certain information from an interview will help you get the job.

Although I strongly discourage you from lying to your prospective employer, there might be things you can embellish or omit certain information in an interview. I'll give you some examples, in no particular order:

1)   Salary. This is the number one thing that people lie about in their interviews. I recommend against this, as it could come back to bite you later, especially if the human resources department from your new company checks your references and the question of your salary comes up. Instead of making up a salary that is higher than you receive in your current position, you might put a price tag on your current compensation package, including salary, vacation time, benefits, etc. i.e.—"I have a compensation and benefits package that I would value near $150,000."

2)   Your talents and abilities. Some people will lie about what they can do. For example, when asked if they are familiar with a particular software program, they might indicate that they are familiar with it when they don't know how to use this. If this is something you can take a crash course on and learn between the interview and your start date, you could probably get away with it. But if you're not familiar with the program and can't learn it quickly, you're going to be in trouble when you are actually on the job and your employer expects you to know how to use the program. You'll be better off being honest and telling the interviewer that you are not familiar with the program, but that you are a fast and willing learner and willing to learn that skill quickly. I knew a graphic designer who lied about the graphic programs he was familiar with. He was hired for the job. But two

Job Interview Preparation

days into the job, his employer figured out that the new employee wasn't familiar with the graphics programs he said he was, and that graphic artist was terminated less than a week into his new job.

3)   How you feel about your current boss or co-workers. This is an area in which you can do some harm to yourself. If you had major conflicts with current or past bosses or co-workers, you will not benefit from trashing them in your interview. No, you certainly don't have to sing their praises, however you won't accomplish anything by trashing them either.

4)   Your greatest weaknesses. If a prospective employer inquires about what your greatest weaknesses are, it's probably OK for you to highlight a weakness other than your greatest weakness. Instead of admitting a weakness that can't be corrected easily, you should select a weakness that you can or maybe have already improved upon. i.e.— "I previously took on more projects than I could handle, without delegating. I realized that shortcoming and have since worked to utilize my team much better. Although, I'm still working on this, I now feel like I've improved to the level where it's no longer a problem."

5)   Who you know. It's OK to drop names during an interview, but make sure that you at least know the person you say you know, as this is yet another thing that can come back to bite you if you lie.

6)   Your interests. If you're asked what your main interests are outside of work, it's probably OK to select lesser interests that make you look better to a prospective employer. Although, beware. I knew a young man who professed that he loved to golf, when he saw golf trophies in the interviewer's office. He didn't golf at all and soon after he was hired, the interviewer kept asking him if he wanted to join in a round of golf. The young man continued to decline, but he told me

that the interviewer who was now his co-worker eventually figured out that the young man was not a golfer and, although the young man wasn't fired, he was embarrassed by the situation.

7) Fired or quit. If you were fired or laid off from your past position, be honest about it, but don't dwell on it. Focus on the positive and tell your employer that you're ready for new challenges and opportunities.

8) Places you've worked. If you've had places you've worked at for short periods of time or places where you had a bad experience, it's OK for you to leave that off your resume or out of the interview conversation, as long as you can explain any employment gaps in your resume.

Again, no one can tell you whether you should lie, embellish, or omit information during your interview. You'll have to determine this based on your ethics and the principles you live by. However, if you do lie or embellish, I strongly suggest that you examine the possible consequences of doing so.

Chapter 8—The Future is Waiting

Your interview is over. You either got the job or you didn't, or you'll have to wait for the prospective employer to make a decision. Either way, there are some things you should do to follow up on your interview.

What to do after the job interview.

Before you hang up the phone, sign off from a video call, or leave the interview, it's extremely important for you to ask the interviewer when to follow up (presuming they didn't announce a decision before the interview ended). If you interviewed with multiple people, find out who you should follow up with and how the interviewer would prefer that you follow up. (Do they want you to call, do they want you to email them?, etc.)

After you've cleared your head, I suggest that you sit down and write or type some notes from the interview. As days pass after an interview, you're likely to forget some of the things that were discussed during the interview and you'll probably find it beneficial to have some notes which you can refer back to, if necessary.

After you've done that, you should plan to send a thank you note to each person you interviewed with. If you had a phone interview or a video interview, an emailed thank you note is appropriate. If you've had a face-to-face interview, I would recommend that you send an email thank you that same day and then a handwritten snail mail thank you that day or the following day. If you are emailing thank you notes to multiple people, write a personal and different note to each person you interviewed with. Preferably not the same note copied. An emailed note will afford you the opportunity to reiterate your interest in the job and emphasize again why you are the right fit for the job.

Job Interview Preparation

The snail mail note should be much shorter, probably on a thank you card of some kind. With both note forms, I recommend that you always thank the interviewers for their time, tell them that you enjoyed learning more about the position and the company, and again express your interest and enthusiasm for the job they are offering.

In sending thank you notes, you should note that you're probably not going to get a job based on a thank you note, but if you don't send a note, you could lose the job. Thank you notes offer applicants the chance to stay "top of mind" with interviewers and if you don't send a thank you not or follow up as agreed upon, the interviewer may well think that you're not interested in the job.

If you are working with a corporate recruiter or a headhunter in your job search, ask your recruiter to follow up with a phone call to the hiring manager. They should be able to find out how you did in the interview. Even if you're working with a recruiter, the thank you notes need to come from you and not the recruiter. The interviewer needs to understand that you're interested in the job, not just that the recruiter is interested in placing you. And, if you're using a recruiter, I suggest that you personally follow up with the interviewer instead of leaving the task solely to the recruiter.

Hopefully, you've made note of when the interviewer asked you to follow up with them. A couple of notes regarding these follow-ups. Follow up when the interview told you to follow up. Not sooner, not later. You may have to walk a fine line between seeming interested in the job and seeming desperate or becoming a nuisance. When following up, ask them for an update on where they are in the hiring process and with each call or email ask them when you should contact them again to get an updated status. And, if it feels appropriate, you might ask them how you are stacking up against the other candidates they've interviewed. If you can get an answer on this, you'll have a better inkling as to what your chances are to get the job.

And while you are waiting to hear on one job, don't let that stop you from searching for other jobs. Depending on what positions you're interviewing for, getting a job can sometimes be a numbers game and there's no harm in interviewing for multiple jobs at the same time. If you get an offer on one job while you're waiting to hear on another job that you would prefer more, you'll then have a decision to make, but that will be a nice problem to have.

You Got the Job! Now what?

Bingo! You got the job! That great news should sets in motion the things you'll need to do to transition from you old job to your new job.

Upon receiving a job offer, you should confirm the offer with a letter of acceptance. In the letter, you should confirm the agreed-upon start date, salary, and entire compensation package (if the employer hasn't already confirmed these things in writing with their offer). Make a copy of your letter of acceptance for future reference if questions should arise later.

Then you will need to tell your current boss that you have accepted a position with another company. You can do this verbally or with a formal letter of resignation. When you are submitting a letter of resignation, you should also copy the human resources person in your company. If you're initially informing your boss of your new job in writing, you should then offer to meet with him or her at their convenience to establish a transition plan. You should know that there are some companies who will not allow you to continue to work there after you've submitted a letter of resignation. Don't take this personally, as some companies have that policy and it shouldn't be taken personally. A client of mine hosts a radio talk show. When he got a job at another station three years ago, station management told him that he would not be allowed on air anymore. He'd worked there for seven years and he took that as a personal affront, disappointed that he would not be allowed to say goodbye to all the people who had loyally listened to his radio show over the years. I told him not to take that personally, as it was simply company policy. (The station was owned by a media conglomerate that had previously been burned by allowing a departing employee to continue on the air waves after that employee had tendered his resignation. The employee proceeded to "trash" the station with lots of negative comments during his final radio show. Thus, there was a reason for the company policy.)

In any letter of resignation or any of your actions following your resignation, I strongly suggest that you take the high road and remain gracious throughout the process, even if you had things about working there that you didn't like. It's never good to burn bridges in leaving a job. That might make you feel better, but it will also show a lack of respect for the people who continue to work there and you never know if you'll need something from one of those people in the future. Any letter of resignation should note that you were happy for the opportunity to work there and that you wish them success in the future (even if you might not).

In meeting with your soon-to-be former boss or supervisor, it will be good if you can agree on a transition plan. Will your supervisor want you to train someone else for the position you're leaving? Will he want you to provide detailed instructions for your replacement? I've had many clients who have been quick to offer their new contact information to their former supervisor, telling them that they are welcome to call any time they have questions regarding the position they left. If you don't think that your previous employer will become a nuisance with lots of phone calls, this is probably OK. However, if you're going to do this, you should be aware that it is possible that your new employer may frown upon this practice and you might want to instruct your old supervisor to contact you after hours. An exception to making such an offer to your old company would be if you've gone to work for a competitor. If this is the case, it's probably not even ethical for you to help your previous company and your new employer is almost sure to frown upon the idea of you helping your old employer.

Throughout the transition process at the company you're leaving, I suggest that you continue to maintain occasional contact with your new company, just to make sure everything continues to be "go". And, if you have any new questions that come up while you are waiting to start your new job, these occasional contacts will be good times to ask those questions of your future employer.

And finally, as you prepare to leave your old job for the new job, I'll remind you once again to "take the high road". Don't diss the company you're leaving, don't flaunt your new job to the co-workers you're leaving behind, and don't coast in your last days there. Continue to work hard, continue to display a positive and grateful attitude, and take the time to thank any people there who were helpful to you. Make the most of your remaining time there and create a smooth and pleasant transition from your old job to the exciting next chapter of your career.

How to Transform a Rejection into Something Positive.

So, you just got the dreaded "we've decided to go in a different direction" news. You're not going to get that job you had wanted so badly. What do you do now?

Well, first you should realize that life isn't all puppy dogs and balloons. We all get rejected at one time or another. One of the most difficult things about being a job applicant is that ultimately whether you get hired is beyond your control. I know people who swear that they did the best they could possibly do and it still wasn't enough to get the job. Some of those people even think they had the perfect interview; there was nothing they could have done better. Maybe they didn't have as much experience as other candidates, maybe they didn't have the skills that other candidates had. Either way, they didn't get the job.

I always encourage people who have been rejected in a job interview to maintain a positive attitude, to continue to focus on the process and not the results, and to look back and analyze the interview to see if there was anything they could have done better or could be doing better.

Here are some suggestions on things you can do after you've been rejected in an interview:

1) Ask for feedback. After you've been told that the company you interviewed with has decided to go in a different direction, ask for their feedback as to why you didn't get the job. Ask this in a positive manner, not a defensive manner, and you might be surprised at how many hiring managers are forthcoming about why you didn't get the job. And, if you are working through a recruiter or headhunter to get a job, the same applies. Ask them to follow up with the employer to see where and why you came up short. You can use this information to evaluate the way you're interviewing. If you get rejected from multiple jobs for the same or similar reasons, you'll probably need to look at how you're interviewing or the positions you're interviewing for.

2) Analyze, identify, and adapt. It's important that you continue to analyze why you're not getting the jobs you're applying for. As mentioned above, if you can get feedback from the people you interviewed with, that will certainly help. But whether you get feedback from interviewers or not, you should constantly be analyzing

Job Interview Preparation

your process and your performance in trying to get the jobs you want. Sure, it's possible that you might not be doing anything wrong at all, however you'll be selling yourself short if you don't at least step back and look for areas you could improve upon in your interviewing efforts.

3)   Focus on things you can change. In some instances, you won't be able to make any changes based on the reason you didn't get the job. For example, I have a client from Illinois who recently applied for a sale position with a national firm. The sales position was responsible for two states, Louisiana and Texas. When my client found out that the company he interviewed with had decided to go in a different direction, he asked the hiring manager if there was a reason they hadn't chosen him. The hiring manager noted that the candidate who was hired, had previous sales experience in those states and that's why they decided to go with him instead of my client. Well, this was something that was certainly beyond my client's control. He couldn't control where his territories were, and he had no knowledge of that going into the interview. Also, it was mere coincidence that the person who got the job had worked previously in those Louisiana and Texas. So, my client probably didn't do anything wrong in his interview process. Someone else was just lucky enough to have worked in those states before.

I'll giving you another story which illustrates how an applicant focused on the shortcomings he could change. A relative of mine is a baseball coach. I get the feeling that he's great at what he does, because I've read about his achievements on the internet. (Everything we read on the internet is true, right? Joke.) Well, for years, my relative had been a community college coach who has been interested to become a minor league batting coach and then eventually work his way up to being a major league batting coach. Over two years, he had interviews with four different minor league baseball teams and each time he came

Job Interview Preparation

away empty. Frustrated, he finally decided to go back to the people he interviewed with and find out why they hadn't hired him and what the differences were between him and the persons they hired. The first two organizations he called were forthcoming enough to tell him that they were concerned with whether he would be able to work well with the Latin American players, as he did not speak Spanish. For those of you that don't know, there are a large percentage of Latin American players in the US minor and major baseball leagues and not all of them speak or understand English proficiently. So, armed with this information, my relative took it upon himself to take some accelerated Spanish classes. Sure enough, by the time the next season came around, he was very competent at speaking Spanish. He applied for a job as a minor league batting coach and he was hired. A couple lessons can be learned from his experience. First, he solicited feedback on why he'd been previously rejected. Second, he analyzed that information and determined that he probably wasn't winning those jobs because he didn't speak Spanish, even though that was never advertised as a requirement for the job. Third, he realized that he could change that deficiency and took some Spanish courses.

4) Promise to learn something from your rejection. It's no secret that we can learn a lot from our failures. And if we don't learn from our failures, we'll keep repeating them. If you've been rejected for a job, take it upon yourself to analyze what you could have done better and learn from it. Otherwise, all of the time and effort you spent preparing for that interview will surely go to waste. Try to take something valuable away from each rejection.

5) Refine your search. With the interview for the job you didn't get, was there anything you didn't like about the jobs or the companies you interviewed with? Rejection aside, maybe you discovered some things about the job or the company that weren't as great as you thought they would be. If so, you might use this information to refine

Job Interview Preparation

your search. As an example, if someone applies for an accounting management job and they realize from the interview that the job requires a lot more managing of people that it does accounting. And the person who applied for this job really isn't interested much in managing people. He would prefer more to be involved in just the accounting aspects of an accounting job. With that self-analysis, he can refine his future searches to accounting jobs that do not include management responsibilities.

6) Focus on the process, not the outcome. My clients will tell you that I harp on the idea that, in looking for a job, they need to focus on the process of going about getting a job and preparing and interviewing well instead of the outcome. Interviewing is a process and you won't be able to control the outcome of who is chosen for the job. However, if you can continue to fine tune the methods you are using to get and prepare for the interviews and continue to analyze and refine the way you're interviewing, you'll give yourself the best chance to manipulate the outcome. So, focus on the process and not the outcome.

Conclusion

So, there you have it. Now that you've read this book, you have the tools to go out and get the interviews you want. You also have some tips and techniques which should help you interview more successfully, be your best self, and land the job you really want.

We've discussed a variety of topics you can use in increase your chances of getting the job. You can get more interviews by using the tips I've given you to build a better resume. You can position yourself above other candidates by writing cover letters that will grab the reader and tell the interviewer why you are someone who is a formidable candidate who they have to interview.

We've discussed how to dress for an interview, how to overcome nervousness and anxiety. We've discussed the importance of doing your homework and researching the company you're interviewing with, so you can avoid the "So, what do you all do here?" question to start your interview. You should also have a better handle on how to navigate difficult questions in an interview and you now know what questions to ask during an interview. You know how to handle questions that catch you off-guard. With the right body language and an air of confidence, you'll be able to stand out and make a killer first impression. You now know what prospective employers want to hear and you know things they don't want to hear. And you know how to follow up after a job interview. If you're fortunate enough to become the leading candidate, you'll know how to negotiate to get the optimum salary. You'll also know what needs to happen after you accept an offer.

Bottom line, you now have the tools in your toolbox to score and ace interviews.

Job Interview Preparation

As I've mentioned before, the job interview process is a competition. You'll be competing against other candidates who have the same goal as you do—to get the job. If you're going to have a chance, you'll have to find a way to stand out from these other candidates. You're going to have to tweak and fine-tune your interview process. Although I've known people who have maintained that they had a perfect interview, but didn't get the job, I've always encouraged those people to continue to go back and analyze their process. Did they really do everything right? Isn't there something they could have improved upon?

Interviewing for a job can be a frustrating process, mostly because it includes some elements that are beyond your control. With the candidates who have felt that they've done everything right throughout the interview process, but still haven't landed the job, I tell them the same thing I'll tell you: In interviewing for jobs, it's important for you to focus on the process of getting the job, not the outcome. You can control what you do in your efforts to get the job, but you can't control whether you get the job. Unfortunately, that's beyond your control. So again, with those things in mind, focus on the process, not the outcome. If you can do that, I assure you that you'll have more success in getting interviews and you'll increase your chances of landing the job.

If you don't get a job, for whatever reason, don't hang your head. If you can learn from your past rejections, those rejections will ultimately help you improve your process. Yes, I have clients who tell me that they're tired of learning from their mistakes. That being said, I always remind them that searching for a new job is often a numbers game. It's a process, not an event. The more and the quicker you can fine-tune your process, the quicker you'll be able to land that new job.

You've now spent some of your valuable time in reading this book. I'm hoping that you'll now take the time to implement immediately some of the tips and techniques I've given you. With many self-help or "how to" books such as this one, readers make the mistake of not resolving to make changes immediately. They'll resolve to make changes someday, whenever they get around to it. Unfortunately, most of those people never get around to it. That's why I encourage you to make changes and change your process immediately. If you are willing to do that, you'll surely enhance your chances of getting the job you want. Although I can't guarantee that you'll get every job you apply for, I can say that if you use the tools I've provided, you'll be able to be your best self in trying to get interviews and you'll have a much better chance to succeed in the interviews you have.

So, let's get after it!

Wishing you more interviews and more interview success. Happy hunting!

www.ingramcontent.com/pod-product-compliance
Lightning Source LLC
Chambersburg PA
CBHW030000110526
44587CB00011BA/924